The Prophet of Carmel

The Life of Elias the Thesbite

The Prophet of Carmel

Written by
Rev. Charles B. Garside, M.A.

Preface by
Rev. Edward F. Garesché, S.J.

Cover Painting of Elias the Prophet
by David Fielding
Copyright 2006

LORETO PUBLICATIONS
Fitzwilliam, NH 03447
AD 2007

𝔑𝔦𝔥𝔦𝔩 𝔒𝔟𝔰𝔱𝔞𝔱:

> C. J. Kluser,
> > *Librorum Censor*

𝔍𝔪𝔭𝔯𝔦𝔪𝔞𝔱𝔲𝔯:

> † Joannes J. Swint,
> > *Epis. Wheelingensis*

April 21, 1924

Published by:

LORETO PUBLICATIONS
P. O. Box 603
Fitzwilliam, NH 03447
603-239-6671
www.LoretoPubs.org

ISBN: 1-930278-50-0

Printed and bound in the United States of America

Table of Contents

Forward

For many years this excellent work by Reverend Charles B. Garside, M.A., has been out of print. A few rare copies were to be found in the libraries of Carmel and of other religious houses, but these were not accessible to the public. It is in compliance with repeated requests that this new edition is presented.

The prophet of Carmel, St. Elias, has ever been regarded by the Carmelites as their leader and founder — a tradition which Holy Church has confirmed in granting to the order a Proper Mass and office of the saint on July 20, and in permitting the erection of his statue in St. Peter's, Rome, among the founders of religious orders, Benedict XIII himself having written the inscription for it: "The Order of Carmel has erected this statue to the holy prophet Elias, its founder."

The history of Elias as recorded in the Old Testament will be found admirably developed in the following pages, and it is devoutly hoped that many readers will carry away from their perusal an efficacious devotion to this great prophet, who was and is so powerful with God.

This is not the place for a detailed account of the children of the Prophet — the glorious Carmelite Order which came forth from the caves of Mount Carmel in Palestine in the thirteenth century to establish innumerable monasteries throughout Europe. It will not be amiss, however, to sketch the progress of the Carmelites in the United States.

In 1790, Carmelite nuns from Antwerp founded in Maryland the first monastery of religious women in our land. Seventeen houses of the nuns are now scattered from coast to coast, including: Baltimore, 1790; St. Louis, 1863; New Orleans, 1877; Boston, 1890; Philadelphia, 1902; Brooklyn, 1907; Seattle, 1908; Santa Clara, 1908; Davenport, 1911; Los Angeles, 1913; Wheeling, WV, 1913; New York, 1919; New Albany, 1922, and Cleveland, 1923. A community of exiled Mexican Carmelites, accorded hospitality at Grand Rapids, has recently branched out to Buffalo and to Schenectady.

The nuns of St. Teresa's Reform preceded their brothers, the Discalced Carmelite Friars, in the United States by more than a century, for it is only within the last twenty years that Fathers from the Bavarian Province assumed charge of a Shrine of Our Lady, near Milwaukee; and Spanish Fathers are now laboring on the missions in Arizona and Oklahoma. In 1916, the College of Our Lady of Mt. Carmel was founded in Washington, D.C., by Fathers from the Province of Catalonia, Spain, as a house of studies affiliated to the Catholic University of America, for the young professed theologians of the order.

The Calced Carmelite Fathers have had houses in New York, Niagara Falls, Englewood, Pittsburgh and Chicago for many years.

In the midst of a world that ignores them, when it does not condemn them, the Carmelites perpetuate the spirit of their leader "who stood up as a fire, and whose words burned as a torch." (Eccl. 48)

Blazoned on their shield, surmounting its flaming, we read the motto of the mighty thesbite, *"Zelo zelatus sum*

Forward

pro Domino Deo exercituum." (With zeal I have been zealous for the Lord God of Hosts) It is this spirit of his, of burning zeal for the glory of God and the salvation of souls, that consumes the elite nun in her silent cloister, making her thus partaker in the apostolic life of the Carmelite friar and equally with him continuing the mission the prophet of old "to appease the wrath of the Lord." (Eccl. 48:10)

Carmel of Wheeling
April, 1924

Preface

When my dear and valued friends, the Discalced Carmelites of Wheeling, wrote to request me to provide a preface for their new edition of Father Garside's work, *The Prophet of Carmel*, I was glad to agree to do so for their sake, if any words of mine could be of service. But after reading the book itself and becoming deeply interested in its contents, I am the more willing to commend it to the reader.

There is a charm and wonder about the life of St. Elias which intrigue the imagination and increase the soul's devotion. Such a singular destiny is here, a career of such extraordinary marvels, that the history of mankind offers no parallel. Even the figures of the prophets of the Old Law, mysterious and wonderful as they are, cannot match in singular privilege this man of God who was seized upon by angels and carried aloft in a chariot of fire, to remain alive in his mortal flesh even to our day and far beyond it, until the distant times when he shall descend on earth to be a martyr for the Faith.

Somewhere, in some state of mortal existence, Elias still lives. He shall so live long after we who now inhabit this earth have perished. During all the Christian era, this man of strange destiny will continue in life until what time it shall please the providence of God to bring him forth from his obscure retirement, still living in the flesh, to preach the word of God to the Jews and to die in witness of his Faith.

The career of Elias, while he still walked among men, was likewise full of poetic beauty, heroism, and the evidence of the divine power. His character of piety and courage, his contempt of luxury and the courts of kings, his unearthly fearlessness in carrying out the hard embassies of God — all these things make him, as Father Garside so often points out in his pages, a model and a lesson for these days as well as for his own simple and primitive times. Human nature remains wonderfully the same. The temptations, the difficulties, the pains and wearinesses of today are mirrored in the world of old where St. Elias moved and spoke. Like all the saints, he has an eloquent message, not to one time only, but to all days. The present volume brings out this message with edifying clearness.

It is true that Father Garside himself belonged to a more simple age than ours. The very paragraphs of his book, couched in a less flexible and familiar style than is popular nowadays, give evidence that he is not a recent author. Yet the interested reader will remark how little change has taken place in the essential problems of humanity since Father Garside's day. The applications which he makes are often as pertinent and as much needed now as they were in his own time.

It is, of course, well known, as the *Foreword* remarks, that St. Elias has long been regarded by the Carmelites as their founder. This pious belief has always been dear to them. Surely the ancient prophet is very near in spirit to the sons and daughters of Carmel. He is, by his great example of austerity and prayer upon the sacred slopes of Mt. Carmel, a singularly providential model to these

Preface

devoted souls who make for themselves a solitude of love and zealous prayer in the midst of an indifferent world. On Carmel are worthy followers and clients of him who, while apart from the world in affection and desire, played so powerful a part in promoting the interests of God's kingdom during his long vigils of prayer on Mt. Horeb and Mt. Carmel.

Edward F. Garesché, S. J.

Introduction

There are, as we all know, different kinds of saints. There are those in whose lives, remarkable though they may be in various ways, we can, nevertheless, recognize much that is perfectly intelligible to the most ordinary mind; much that, pointing suggestively to our own individual position, duties, trials and graces, we can set before us, as an ideal at least, for our personal imitation. When we read about these saints, we feel as if it were possible to have boldness and trustfulness enough to put our tiny hands into their kindly grasp, and to endeavor to toil on, at all events for a short distance, in the sweet company of their example. In tracing what may be termed the geographical line of their spiritual journey, we meet, indeed, frequently with lofty peaks and profound depths where we and they must necessarily part; but it may be said that they attract and encourage rather than astonish or dismay. They are undoubtedly brilliant stars in the firmament of righteousness, but they move in a higher orbit far above the less brilliant luminaries.

It was said of Saul, the son of Cis, that "he stood in the midst of the people, and he was higher than any of the people from the shoulders upwards." (1King 10:23) And so these saints are conspicuous for their spiritual stature, but there is, notwithstanding, sufficient in common between them and many inferior servants of God to enable

The Prophet of Carmel

them to be claimed by the latter, without gross presumption, as their brethren. However high they stand in comparison with others, still they may be described, in a limited yet true sense, as belonging to "the people."

There are other saints whose names, when uttered, place at once between them and ourselves an immeasurable distance. They appear to have been cast in a mold altogether different from our own humanity and, as we walk around and contemplate their majestic forms, we are conscious of that fact at every step of our reverent survey. They are giants amongst giants; between their past career and the possibilities of our own we perceive scarcely a single point of contact and resemblance; everything within and around them was both uncommon and on a vast scale. On entering the very portals of the biography of some of them we seem to be passing instantly through the gates of another world.

If it be asked to which of the two classes Elias ought to be assigned, the answer unquestionably is, to the latter. He lived, indeed, under that dispensation of the Old Law which, although "glorious," (2 Cor. 3:7) was after all only a "shadow of the good things to come." (Heb. 10:1) We see him only by glimpses, but it is impossible to follow attentively his brief history, so far as it is disclosed to us in the pages of the sacred volume, without feeling that every glimpse is a revelation of wonderful grandeur, a grandeur of virtues, of deeds, of individual character and of supernatural powers. There is something so heroic, so awe inspiring about him, that by many persons it will be probably supposed that, in choosing Elias amongst other saints of the Old Testament for the subject of our reflections in the present work, we have selected a field not likely to be very fertile in practical instruction for the present day.

Introduction

We believe that this supposition will prove to be unfounded. There is one point which it will be useful to remember — the purpose for which all such inspired accounts of the great saints of God as we possess have been originally composed and preserved in an imperishable record. They have not, like some secular biographies, been given to the world in order to satisfy a useless or unworthy curiosity, but to promote edification. They are not history embroidered with romance; i.e., compositions in which the real and the imaginative have been artistically interwoven for the purpose of relieving, by unexpected contrasts of light and shade, vivid coloring and a variety of fanciful illustrations, materials which would have been otherwise dry and monotonous, although in the main true. On the contrary, they are not only infallibly accurate both in substance and detail, but they are spiritual and practical in their general aim. They do not merely stereotype facts for the intellect, but they are intended to influence the heart. "All Scripture, inspired of God, is profitable to teach, to reprove, to correct, to instruct in justice, that the man of God may be perfect, furnished to every good work." (2 Tim. 3:16,17) All the accounts of the saints, therefore, which are contained in the scriptures (St. Paul, in the above passage, is pointedly referring to the Old Testament, in which Timothy had been instructed from his infancy) were written in order to promote the sanctification of man. They do not owe their origin to any accidental circumstances or to any human design. They have been handed down to posterity by the command of God. Thus the rays which were shed upon the world in long-past ages by the glorious conduct of such saints have been gathered together and fixed in a sacred and immortal lamp for the perpetual illumination of the lowest, as well as the highest, of the children of men in every land and age.

The Prophet of Carmel

Even the vocations, miracles and events that characterized the most extraordinary amongst the spiritual heroes
mentioned in the holy scriptures are pregnant with lessons
of high practical value for ourselves. Their lives were not
merely stupendous exhibitions of divine power moving in
and working through a mortal framework without annihi-
lating it by so tremendous a presence. They were not
intended simply to be gazed upon with that mingled fascination of curiosity and awe with which we look upon
unusually striking manifestations of creative power and
beauty in the earth and heavens. They were, indeed,
mighty handwritings traced by the finger of God upon the
souls of those whom He had especially chosen thus to
honor, but they were also spiritual maps and charts,
although on a gigantic scale, which the most insignificant
among us can even now contemplate with advantage.

Elias's introduction to the reader's notice in the Old
Testament is singularly abrupt. He starts up in the pages
of the sacred volume with a suddenness strikingly akin
to that of his first appearance before Achab, king of
Israel. He is described as "Elias the Thesbite of the
inhabitants of Galaad." (3 King 17:1) These words are
an allusion, according to the general opinion of commentators, to the place of his nativity; but whether he was
called "Elias the Thesbite" from Thisbe in Nepthali,
and, therefore, was only a settler amongst the
Galaadites, or whether he was born in some part of
Galaad bearing at that time a name similar to Thisbe, is
a still controverted question of biblical interpretation.

Beyond the above mentioned slight indication, not a syllable is told us of the antecedents of his life before the
commencement of his great career as a prophet of God.[6]
We can picture to ourselves a Moses floating, unconscious

Introduction

of danger in his boat cradle of papyrus, on the waters of the Nile; or a Samuel sleeping a child's slumber near the aged dim-sighted Heli "in the temple of the Lord, where the ark was . . . before the lamp of God went out;" or a David, "ruddy and beautiful to behold, and of a comely face," watching with his young bright eyes the flock of his father Jesse in the pastures of Bethlehem; but we have no materials for tracing the Thesbite from a lesser point to a greater, from an acorn to the full-grown oak. About his parentage and early years holy scripture preserves a complete silence.

---

[6] St. Epiphanius, in his Lives of the Prophets, relates that when the mother of Elias gave him birth, his father, Sobac, beheld this vision: men carrying a white garment before them paid homage to the child whom they tore from his mother's breast and cast into the fire, feeding him with flames instead of milk. (Brev. Carm. die xx Jul.)

Mount Carmel from the Sea

Chapter One
The King and the Prophet

Vivit Dominus Deus Israel, in cujus conspectu sto, si erit annis his ros et pluvia, nisi juxta iris mei verba.

"As the Lord liveth, the God of Israel, in whose sight I stand, there shall not be dew nor rain these years, but according to the words of my mouth." — 3 Kings 17:1

Elias comes before us surrounded with the glory of an extraordinary mission, fulfilled by him with dauntless fidelity, under circumstances of peculiar difficulty and danger.

At the time when we first hear of him, Achab, the son of Amri, was king of the ten tribes which, after their rebellious separation from Juda, went collectively by the name of Israel. "Now Achab the son of Amri reigned over Israel in the eight and thirtieth[1] year of Asa, king of Juda." (3 King 16:29) No description can sum up the character of Achab with more withering conciseness than the following words: "Achab did more to provoke the Lord the God of Israel than all the kings of Israel that were before him." (3 King 16:33) The evil path of Jeroboam, the first king of the revolted tribes, was too narrow in its lawlessness for him; the golden calves, which had been erected by Jeroboam at Dan and Bethel, represented a religion too much akin to that of the true God to content Achab. "It was not enough for him to walk in the sins of Jeroboam the son of Nabat, but he also took to wife Jezabel, daughter of Ethbaal, king of the Sidonians." (3 King 16:31) In consequence of this marriage with the daughter of an idolatrous heathen, he became the slave of two debasing superstitions, the worship of Baal and of Astaroth; the former the male, and the latter the female divinity of the Phoenicians.

[1] B. C. 918.

1

The Prophet of Carmel

Nor was it sufficient for Achab to plunge his own soul and body in these abominations, or to practise his impiety in secret. He was the public defender, the open patron, the zealous propagator of this plague throughout the whole land over which his sceptre swayed.

Before this man, accustomed to the flattering incense of a corrupt court and with an army at his call, Elias suddenly appears. The king has not sent for him; it is he who has sought out the king. We can visualize the gaunt form of the solitary, fresh from the stern gorges of Galaad; his dark locks hanging in massive clusters over his shoulders, a leathern girdle encircling his spare loins, and his only armor a cape of rough sheepskin for a defense against the elements, and, perhaps, a simple mountain staff in his hands. How weak he seems to a military eye, and yet how strong he really is with an invisible might! Quick to cross the path of Achab, quickly he begins and ends his task. He has no time to waste in idle ceremony; he has a message to deliver. Hardly has Achab begun to scan his figure with mingled feelings of curiosity and contempt, and then of vague misgivings, when these startling words fall upon his ear: "As the Lord liveth, the God of Israel, in whose sight I stand, there shall not be dew nor rain these years but according to the words of my mouth." (3Kng. 17:1) An ordinary man charged with this message would probably have faltered in his speech, and pleaded that he was merely the mechanical mouthpiece of an authority for whose decrees he was not responsible. A diplomat would have softened down the unexpected severity of the message by ingenious phrases redolent of ambiguity and courtesy. A timid man, recognizing the dignity and power of Achab's position, and the certain peril of death as a rapid consequence of such a denunciation, would have fled even before opening his lips.

Elias was of another stamp. "He stood up," says the author of *Ecclesiasticus*, "as a fire." (Eccu. 48:1) This is a striking figure of comparison, for a fire respects nothing. It has no reserves or distinctions. It follows its own law with unerring directness, and consumes whatever meets its path, whether it be vile or precious. It laps up with its devouring tongue the most gorgeous palaces as well as the meanest cabins. It is also a ruthless exposer of the outward, the flimsy, the temporary and the mendacious. It probes as it burns; it "tries every man's work," and only pauses before something stronger than itself. So Elias stood up as a column of fire before Achab; he was there to flash upon him an irresistible prophecy, and to scorch him with a terrible judgment. To all human appearance, the royal idolator, at whose feet numbers were daily bowing themselves to the dust, was the real embodiment of force. He had but to clap his hands, and numerous slaves would spring to his side; but before the prophet of God, he was in fact frailer than a reed, and his royalty and pomp were but the wretched covering of a religious and moral rottenness never before witnessed in Israel.

Why was this living column of fire so bright, so calm, so victorious? Because Elias was preeminently a man of faith. He saw by a clear, inward, supernatural light the naturally invisible. Those grand realities which, when thoroughly discerned, surpass, displace and eclipse everything else, were always present before the eyes of his soul. The objects which the senses supply from the world of sense were to him unsatisfying and unimpressive. If at any moment visions of earthly grandeur or pleasure rose up before his fancy, they were detected at once as illusions. Such images were like those airy, tinted, gossamer clouds which sail rapidly sometimes over the face of the sky, and as they pass along only serve to bring out, with new distinctness and brilliancy the calm glory of the deep, unchangeable heavens.

By faith, Elias beheld with an infallible accuracy and keenly conscious assurance the unity of the true God, the beautiful sanctity of His law, the majestic wisdom and harmony of His government, the watchful and fatherly tenderness of His mercy. It is one of the priceless virtues of faith, that by bringing divine realities before us, and showing us their value and proportion, it defends us against the imposition of the false and unsubstantial. Faith erects a tribunal within the soul before which all things are analyzed, measured and judged. Truth sits there in permanent possession of the temple, and every idol of error which attempts to enter falls down at the threshold. They who have a lively, vigorous faith, united with charity, "bear God in the body," (1Cor. 6:20) as St. Paul says, wherever they go. They move securely, because they are not puzzled and entangled by the phantoms with which they come in contact as they pass along through an illusory world.

What was Achab in the judgment of Elias? Nothing but a rebel against his Creator, a crowned slave of evil passions. Human respect would have whispered, "He is one who has life and death in his hands; take care not to offend his dignity. Jezabel is notoriously vindictive, beware of her anger. Baal is in fashion at the court; his priests are numerous, and public opinion is all on his side. Look at the incense smoking from numerous altars; look at the housetops, from how many of them do the voices of his votaries rise! Look at the groves, thick with images, and crowded with festal processions in honor of the moon goddess Astaroth. Better leave its people alone, and retire sorrowful to the quiet of the hills of Galaad. How can an insignificant individual like you, without rank or influence, chastise the fanaticism of a king, and dissolve the spell that has enchained his people in the same delusion?"

To all such plausible considerations Elias was stone blind. His faith saw only a horror to be execrated, an evil to be denounced and a testimony to the Living God to be delivered. As it saw, so it spoke, for true courage is the child of true and living faith.

Where faith is weak, where it is not habitually acted upon but is brought out only occasionally, under the influence of a kind of religious politeness, just to prove to ourselves our own orthodoxy, there cannot be boldness in grappling with difficulties.

Where faith is of this kind, its objects have little power over us. They are like the dim, cold images of mountains looming spectrally through a mist; we hardly know which is mountain and which is mist; they are not landmarks which direct our path. If the proper objects of faith lie vaguely in the background, it is certain that other objects will occupy the foreground; or the lines and barriers between the two will not be distinct. Earthly motives and principles will mingle with heavenly motives and principles, and as there will be confusion in our mind, there will necessarily be instability in our conduct. When we do not see the leading objects clearly, our heart beats languidly and our feet tread nervously. Men who believe a lie firmly are often bolder than those who believe a truth feebly. The former have a mark; they know at what they are aiming, and they are not disturbed and distracted by the presence of counter considerations. Their false faith is a force, not by virtue of the error or iniquity to which they cling, but of the clearness and singleness of their vision.

This is a thought especially worthy of our consideration in these days. The world and the devil were never so successful as they are now in pretentiously disguising error under the garb of truth. Vices are enshrined as virtues in the attractive temple of fashion. Immorality is idealized by the magic of eloquently sensuous poetry, so as to seem the spontaneous impulse of innocent nature. Debased views of God and His creation, of the soul and the body, are openly professed in circles of rank and intellect. "Jeroboam made priests of the lowest of the people,"(3Kng. 12:31) but now, many who are recognized for their position and acquirements have become the priests of various idolatries, such as the worship of external nature, of culture, of art, of state government, of liberty, of material force and of humanity in the abstract.

False doctrine is not only tolerated in the "high places" of social life, but its seductive music echoes through "the groves" dedicated especially to what is termed, as if in satire, "sound learning." Presumptuous scepticism is canonized by popular acclamation, as not only a right but a duty and the very perfection of mental and moral freedom. Even the heathenism of ancient Greece and Rome has its apologists, who sigh over its loss as over a departed glory, and delight in wreathing its tomb with their falsely sentimental panegyrics.

While all that was gross in its theory and practice is skillfully passed over in silence, its aesthetical side is unduly magnified. The language of these admirers is sometimes so eulogistic as to suggest the insinuation that paganism was in some points superior to Christianity, and that out of its unhallowed bones might perhaps be extracted in this twentieth century an *elixir vitae*, which would do something towards the regeneration of the world in its old age.

These are some of the hostile elements with which our present life is perilously charged. How can this array of foes be successfully met without clear-sighted and persevering courage and how can this courage be obtained? Certainly it will not spring up by chance out of the ground on which we stand; neither will natural temperament nor routine education supply it. What we require is an atmosphere from which the soul's nerves shall be able to draw a constant current of moral vigor. Faith can create this atmosphere, but it must be no sickly, commonplace, flickering faith. If we only give a glance now and then at the invisible world and its realities; if, moreover, that glance comes from eyes upon whose moral retina this world and its falsehoods have steadily and for a long time been stereotyping their images, our faith will be unequal to the task.

Every Christian is bound, according to his means and opportunity, to confront, denounce and resist the enemies of God. Some have to do it in one way, some in another. The war has to be waged by speech, by writing, by protests, by authority, by active and passive opposition, by sufferings and by various other modes which need not be mentioned in detail. No class is exempt from military service in the great conflict which is perpetually raging. All are called to the ranks, no matter what may be their individual temperament or temptations. The duty lies upon the young just stepping into the maze of the great world, and easily deceived through their natural impressibility; upon the diffident, who are afraid of asserting even the truth too loudly; upon the amiable, who shrink from ruffling any person's serenity; upon the ignorant, who are easily silenced by the learning, real or assumed, of their superiors in general education; upon the poor, whose temptation is to bow down before wealth; upon the idle, who are inclined to give way to almost any usurpation for the sake of peace; and upon the busy, who, being too much occupied with secular cares to apply their minds to things of the soul, leave the battle of heaven and hell to be fought by a deputy instead of by themselves. All are bound, more or less, to "stand up in the sight of God" against the evils of the day. The task is great because these evils are not branded as pestilential by a general condemnation, but are, on the contrary, presented at court and weightily supported by the very influences to which the various classes of Christians are most exposed. The contest is as unavoidable as it is difficult, but with the grace of God we shall succeed if we are "strong in faith." "This is the victory that overcometh the world, even your faith." (Jn. 5:4)

Our adversaries may surpass us in station, talent and accomplishments. They may be clothed in them from head to foot, and we may, like Elias, be alone and unarmed with their weapons, but we shall be the real "men of God." We shall deliver our message without quivering; and though our personal Achab, whoever he may be, may refuse to believe in our words, we shall nevertheless have borne testimony to the true God; and as we retire from our work, the kingdom of evil will confess to having felt a heavy blow.

What has been said hitherto refers to faith in a general sense, but there is one particular act of faith, the habitual practice of which is of immense assistance to the soul whenever fearlessness is required in order to enable it to do its duty.

The King and the Prophet

When the prophet shot the keen arrow of his prediction against the King of Israel, he appealed to the "living God," and pledged his authority as a guarantee for the certainty of its fulfillment, and then he added these solemn words: ". . . in whose sight I stand . . ." Elias, when speaking, stood close to Achab; the two were face to face; but there was another presence, a presence felt by Elias to be inexpressibly nearer and more real than that of the king, a presence unseen by the bodily eyes of either, and yet enveloping and penetrating both with the awful infinity and subtlety of its essence. Did not Elias stand in the sight of Achab? Did he not see him distinctly, so distinctly as to read in his looks the impression made upon his mind by his prophecy? True, but who or what was Achab when regarded in contrast with the presence of God? A point scarcely arresting the attention, an atom of dust, a tiny leaflet too weak to make a rustle in the air as it falls to the ground. How the most exalted earthly greatness, power and distinction dwindle to a phantom when the mind calmly places them within the circle of that "white light" which issues forth even from the thought of the presence of the Living God! What mighty strength, what pure consolation, what calm flowing forth from an indescribable sense of security, what inspiriting encouragement should we obtain, if we adverted frequently and vividly to this sublime fact, the presence of God? Why is it that we often feel in the midst of our duties so much depression of heart? Why is it that difficulties loom so portentously large before us, and that we seem to be in some degree under the judgment pronounced against the wicked, ". . . trembling for fear where no fear was?" (Ps. 52:6) Why is it that our struggles and pains are so needlessly multiplied? Undoubtedly one principal cause is

9

that we so often forget the presence of God. We see our foes; we see our own selves; we see the cost of our sacrifices for the sake of righteousness; but we do not realize that we are, during every moment of this time, unspeakably near to God Himself. It is not sufficient to know this fact in a bare, dry, intellectual way, as we hold some abstract truth which need not have any influence upon our conduct. We must open our mind and heart to its influence; we must have our consciousness in a state of perpetual contact with the reality; our soul must be always stretching out into the Infinite Presence. Men who are benumbed cannot feel an atmosphere of heat, although they are surrounded by its warmth. We must not only "stand in the sight of God," which we all do, whether we advert to it or not, but each of us must say to himself habitually: "However weak I may be naturally, yet I stand ever in the sight of the Omnipotent God, and His might must pour itself into me if I seek to do His will." "Fear not, for I am with thee; turn not aside, for I am thy God . . . Behold, all that fight against thee shall be confounded and ashamed; they shall be as nothing." (Isa. 41:10)

There is a suggestiveness in the little word "stand" which should not escape notice. If any one described himself in a mental colloquy as "standing in the sight of God," he ought to mean something of this kind: "I stand," that is to say, "I am not lying down in idleness or sleep, but I am awake and at my post. I am looking eagerly for the slightest indication of the divine will. I stand, for I am nothing but an unprofitable servant, in the presence of my Master. I am also ready to go promptly wherever I may be sent, to bear any burden that may be placed upon my shoulders, and to resist manfully any assaults that may be made against my soul or the honor of my God."

The King and the Prophet

We have said that a strong habitual sense of the presence of God has a powerful bearing upon the soul as a fortifying influence. If this be the case, we can understand how valuable must be the practice of all actions which imply or proclaim that presence. Short aspirations, such as "O God, I know that Thou art here and seest me"; external gestures of reverence, such as kneeling, prostrating and crossing ourselves; works of piety begun in the Name of the Holy Trinity; the commending of ourselves and others to God's fatherly care; all these and similar practices have, besides their own especial object and reward, the indirect result of accustoming the soul and the whole man to feel the blessed nearness of God. They lower the heavens for us, so that the celestial tabernacle which is above lengthens its mystical cords and, enlarging its folds, encompasses the very globe on which we live with its consoling light and protection.

All trials, sorrows and agonies of the heart, if they lead us more than ever to fly to God for refuge, intensify our sense of His nearness. The more we cling to and lean upon Him, the deeper and more penetrating becomes our consciousness of His all-watchful eye and tender touch. "Seek, and ye shall find" is the secret of a divine philosophy; for real seeking of God is the actual finding of Him, the condition and the reward go together. God often chastises us, or allows strange and unexpected troubles to flow over those little earthly "gardens of delights," where we have vainly prided ourselves upon our homegrown flowers, in order that through the bitter experience of their fleeting beauty we may seek Him who alone is our one and perfect Good. The loss of the creature transforms itself into the presence of the Creator, and from His presence we inhale supernatural vigor, so that the Apostle's words become applicable,

11

The Prophet of Carmel

"When I am weak, then am I powerful." 2Cor. 12:10)

Painful trials not only make us realize God's presence by casting us upon Him for support, but they effect this purpose also in another way. Affliction is the thorn hidden in something to which we are attached. It is the wrench of pain felt on the separation of soul or body from that into which one or the other has planted deeply its roots. This rending of a close fellowship strips the soul of what has been for a long time a second self, and creates around it a region of solitude. The old voices are hushed; the old forms are vanished; sometimes the shock is so severe that the soul reels and staggers through the want of its usual companionship. It has hitherto lived in certain outward things now dead, and it finds itself suddenly alone, rocking to and fro, and feeling about for a new center of balance. If this soul understands and accepts humbly its nakedness, if it cries out of the depths to the Lord, then it begins to perceive the divine presence. Hearing nothing, discerning nothing of its former friends, it flutters out of its weakness and darkness into the "everlasting arms," there to grow strong by remaining still.

This result will only happen if we use our involuntary desolation as God intends that it should be used. To sit in the midst of our ruined joys, and sullenly brood upon our losses, to attempt to reclothe ourselves in the garments that have slowly moldered away, or been suddenly burnt to ashes, or, what is worse, to devise rebellious schemes for replanting and repeopling the waste with its former vanities — such a course will increase our weakness instead of our strength. As there is a soul stillness in which we hear more distinctly than ever the voice of God, so there is another kind of stillness in which the divine voice is silent, and the mental ear is filled only by the sound of the selfish beatings of our own narrow heart. There is a night in which the heavens hang out prominently those golden lamps which are hidden during the garish day, and there is a night which is nothing but darkness. When God in His fatherly mercy leads us into the desert, in order that "we may be still, and know that He is God," blessed are we if we resign ourselves to His will. Then our "wilderness shall rejoice and shall flourish like the lily; it shall bud forth and blossom, and shall rejoice with joy and praise." (Isa. 35:1, 2) "If you return and be quiet, you shall be saved: in silence and in hope shall your strength be." (Isa. 30:10)

Chapter Two
The Drought

Elias . . . oravit ut non plueret super terram, et non pluit annos tres et menses sex.

"Elias . . . prayed that it might not rain upon the earth and it rained not for three years and six months."
— James 5:17

"As the Lord liveth, the God of Israel, in whose sight I stand, there shall not be dew nor rain these years, but according to the words of my mouth." (3Kng. 10:7) [1] This language is luminously clear and peremptorily decisive. It is that of a man who is as sure of the fulfillment of the prediction as if the future event had actually happened. It is remarkable also for the unhesitating boldness with which the speaker appeals to God as a witness, not only that there shall be a drought, but that its duration shall be dependent upon himself. " . . . there shall not be dew nor rain these years, but according to the words of my mouth."

Elias acts as if he were much more than a passive instrument of the Creator, much more than His messenger. His words imply the idea that God had, in some sense, and over a limited region, waived the exercise of His sovereign rights, and put provisionally the direction of the very elements into the hands of one of His creatures. Nor do the words of the prophet mean anything less; for when he said, " . . . there shall not be dew nor rain these years,

---

1. This marvelous power over the elements, by which Elias was given to share, as it were, the omnipotence of their Creator, has caused him to be invoked in seasons of drought and flood. In the Carmelite Order there are recorded many instances of his miraculous intervention in such cases, one of the most famous being that of the great drought at Rome in 1779. (Editor's note.)

but according to the words of my mouth," he was not only reading off, as it were, the future by a supernatural power of prophetical vision, he was claiming to be the controller of that future. He was himself setting the hour upon the dial to which he was pointing. The forces of the earth and the heavens were to await his will, and to move or stop according to his behest. How had Elias obtained this extraordinary power, about which he speaks with such confidence?

The explanation is not given in that particular passage of the narrative in the *Book of Kings* which records the words of the prophet, but we find it mentioned in the New Testament, nearly three thousand years after the event, in illustration of the efficacy of the supplications of the righteous. "The continual prayer of a just man," writes St. James, "availeth much. Elias was a man passible like unto us; and with prayer he prayed that it might not rain upon the earth, and it rained not for three years and six months." (Jas. 5:17) The threat of Elias, which probably sounded to the ears of Achab as the excess of presumption and folly, was in reality a divinely authorized message and the calm victory cry of prayer. How mysterious, as well as mighty, was the result of that just man's pleading with his God! If any chance traveler had seen Elias, when he was in the act of offering up that particular supplication, if he had watched him, as he is described on another occasion, "casting himself down upon the earth, and putting his face between his knees," (3Kng. 18:44) how little would he have dreamed of the forces that would be set in motion by that prostration of a solitary worshiper! What link was there between his few fleeting words and the blight or welfare of a kingdom! And yet when Elias rose from the ground, he knew that his prayer had turned into a decree that would be irresistibly obeyed: " . . . there shall not be dew nor rain these years, but according to the words of my mouth." The judgments of God are various, and in many of them there is an obvious significance. He brands with an unmistakable lesson those whom He burns, so that the cautery itself becomes a language.

Adam, not content with the exquisite, abundant and spontaneous products of the Garden of Eden which his Creator had allowed him to gather, partook of the one fruit which alone of all the rest he was forbidden to eat. What was the result? He was condemned to exile and misery, "cursed is the earth in thy work; with labor and toil shalt thou eat thereof." (Gen. 3:17) He expected by his crime to enjoy Eden more completely, and "the Lord God sent him out of the paradise of pleasure to till the earth from which he was taken." (Gen. 3:24) He yearned for more knowledge, and instantly lost that highest wisdom which he had before possessed, "the wisdom that is from above." He aspired to greater liberty, and he was instantly sentenced to die. He craved for the deification of his being ("Ye shall be as gods." Gen. 3:5), and he ruined himself and the whole human race.

The builders of the tower of Babel impiously perverted to an unsanctified ambition their community of language, and as a punishment and perpetual memorial of the sin, God shattered that unity which had been their temptation; so that the "children of Adam" not only were themselves "scattered abroad into all lands," but they proclaimed, by their fragmentary speech, wherever they went, the fact and origin of their confusion. Gen. 11:9)

The plagues of Egypt were not merely a terrible affliction, but in some of them — the turning of the Nile, for instance, into blood; "so that the fishes that had been in the river died" and the loathsome multiplication of frogs — Pharaoh and his people could not avoid perceiving an irresistible and divinely sarcastic condemnation of their false worship; for the river itself, and many of its fish, as also the frog, were held in sacred veneration. Hence, as it is said in reference to these plagues: "Thou hast greatly tormented them, who in their life lived foolishly and unjustly, by the same things which they worshiped." (Wis. 12:23)

Core, Dathan and Abiron, with their adherents, rebelled against the authority of Moses. They ventured, with a fatal audacity, to offer incense to God; and scarcely had the unhallowed smoke ceased to ascend, when "a fire coming from the Lord destroyed the two hundred and fifty men that offered the incense." (Num.16:35) King David, moved by the spirit of pride, made a census of his subjects, and in three days seventy thousand fell under the Angel of Pestilence. (2Kng. 24:15) Jeroboam stretched forth his hand to seize a prophet of God who had been sent to rebuke him, and "the hand which he stretched forth against him withered, and he was not able to draw it back to him again. (3Kng. 17:24)

Nabuchodonosor said: "Is not this the great Babylon which I have built to be the seat of the kingdom, by the strength of my power; and in the glory of my excellence?" and his next dwelling was with "cattle and wild beasts," and "he did eat grass like an ox." (Dan. 4:27)

These are a few amongst numerous examples of that instructive significance of many of God's chastisements which are easily recognizable by even the cursory reader of the holy scriptures. So also there was a peculiar fitness in the nature of Achab's chastisement, which we shall miss unless

The Drought

we advert to the character of his idolatry. Baal was regarded as the deity especially presiding over the material powers of nature. The name of Baal represents, it is said, the idea of absolute ownership rather than directive guidance. He was the imaginary king whom the earth and the seasons obeyed as his willing slaves. The fertility or barrenness of the soil, the rivers, the dew and rainfall, clouds and sun rays, were considered to be exclusively within his sphere. A punishment, therefore, inflicted by nature herself, as if avenging the dishonor done to her own real Creator, the God of Israel, was a direct blow at the worship of the false god. The day that witnessed the beginning of the drought witnessed also to the impotence of Baal, who was thus proved to be utterly unable to cause it to cease even for a moment. Moreover, if it was bitter enough for Achab to hear the power of Baal ignored, it was still more galling for him to see the apparently insignificant quarter from which the defiance came. It was not the God of Israel, Himself, who in some visible form or by an audible voice, or through the ministry of an angel, proclaimed the nothingness of Baal. It was a man of flesh and blood, "passible," like Achab himself; a man who had neither temple nor images, neither priests nor retinue; a solitary man, with nothing about him outwardly to guarantee the truth of his speech. Such was the person who challenged Baal upon his own special domain, and by conquering him with his own professed weapons, thus forced upon Achab's mind a bitter contrast between the felt reality of the true God and the impotence of the false god.

Besides Baal, the sungod of the Phoenicians, Achab, Jezabel and their people adored Astaroth, the corresponding moon goddess. The details of the worship of these two deities are not clearly known, but it is beyond dispute that they were not less distinguished by festive revelry and

The Prophet of Carmel

unusual splendor of pompous ceremonial than by the grossest sensuality. A chastisement was therefore needed which would seal up many of the sources of material, luxurious enjoyment, and fling upon the riotous hearts of these devotees of a voluptuous fanaticism the stern gloom of daily physical want. As all were guilty, all were made to feel the scourge, without distinction of sex or rank.

There was something, it must be admitted, peculiarly crushing and depressing in the particular punishment upon Achab and his people.

When armed foes clash together in sanguinary strife; when mighty rivers, suddenly bursting their barriers, thunder along in their wild course; or when the flames of a conflagration, rushing to and fro, crackle and roar over their prey — there is much to excite and distract as well as to oppress. The misery is a crisis which summons, as with a trumpet call, all our energies into immediate action. The bold and brave rise with the occasion, and often find in their mind, will and nerves a reserve of unexpected fortitude, of moral force, which, but for the touchstone of the common calamity, would have remained unrevealed and undeveloped.

But drought, with famine in its wake, has a dreadfulness of its own; nature pines day by day, and seems to recoil from any fellowship with man. Its life ebbs slowly yet surely away, until all things are encircled by an awful monotony of barrenness and solitude. There is nothing tangible to grasp, nothing with which to fight the battle of existence; without a sound or visible cause the deadly spell silently works. "The word of Elias," says the writer of Ecclesiasticus, "was a torch." It was indeed a torch, searching and tremendous in its operation. Scarcely did the echoes of the prophet's voice last a moment, and yet

The Drought

in that brief space of time the imperial word was caught
up by the listening earth and sky, and its command was
obeyed. The torch of the word of Elias flashed at once
above, below and around, as if omnipresent. It touched
the heavens, and they became as fiery brass. It touched
the earth, and its fertile bosom shrank and withered.
During three years and six months not a drop of dew or
rain moistened its dryness. The corn fields no longer rip-
pled with their former golden sheen, as the playful breeze
swept over their surface, for the grain that had already
sprung up died prematurely, and the seed that was cast
by the sower into the furrows knew no resurrection. The
vine, olive, fig, pomegranate and other fruit-bearing trees
only mocked the eyes of their owners as the seasons,
recalling to memory their now-vanished productiveness,
came and went in vain. The brooks flowed more and more
languidly, their voices growing fainter and fainter, until
at last they became dumb and perished.

Intense must have been the sufferings of all classes, but
especially of the young, the aged, the poor and the sick in
that stricken land, when, according to the very words of
our Lord Himself, "in the days of Elias . . . there was a
great famine." (Lk. 4:25) An incident, which we shall have
presently to narrate, will unfold some of the heart-rending
miseries of that drought, with a pathetic force and simplic-
ity more graphically effective than any picture which the
imagination can supply.

In the meantime, let us observe what the prophet did
immediately after delivering his message to Achab. It
would have seemed most natural for him to have retired to
some safe refuge beyond the boundary line of the region of
the malediction. Why should he, the executor of the divine
law, be exposed to any of the penalties deserved by the

21

guilty? Why should the sword of justice wound the hand of its legitimate bearer?

Elias, however, followed no human impulses, and consulted no suggestions of worldly prudence. "The word of the Lord came to him: Get thee hence, and go towards the east, and hide thyself by the torrent of Carith, which is beyond the Jordan;" (3Kng. 17:2,3) and without an inquiry or a shadow of hesitation he retired, probably to some cave near that stream. Mark his faith and trust! He goes where there is no civilized dwelling place, to a lonely spot where there is nothing to enliven his solitude except the murmur of a mountain brook, and even its voice becomes less and less as the waters decrease; whilst at night the stillness would often be harshly broken by the restless tramping and fierce howling of wild beasts, upon whom the drought was heavily pressing. Achab, moreover, is seeking everywhere to seize and slay him, but the prophet is without alarm. In that rude cave, which is both his refuge, his home and his oratory, he is far happier than if he were dwelling in the most luxurious mansion. But will he not perish from want? The torrent, so long as it flows, will quench his thirst; whence, however, will the necessary sustenance come? Is there not a risk of his sinking, Samson-like, under the very ruin which his own power has caused? Will he not be consumed by the desolating fire of his own torch? Behold the wonderful and merciful thoughtfulness of that Father without whose permission not even a little sparrow falls to the ground! Morning and evening a welcome rustling of wings through the air heralds to Elias the approach of aid, and two ravens, with punctual obedience to an inspired commission, bring to him bread and meat. These winged messengers of charity are the only living creatures by

The Drought

whose presence the solitude of Elias is cheered; they have not articulate speech, but their unfailing arrivals and their gifts tell of a mystery of providence and love, into whose depths even the divinely illumined eye of the prophet could pierce but a little way. What a bond of singularly touching sympathy must these visits have woven between Elias and his dumb visitors! How faithful they were in bringing to him, untouched, what their natural instinct would have tempted them to devour! Upon how frail and uncertain a thread did his life seem to depend! Yet he never feared that it would break, although supported by two such apparently weak instruments as birds of the air!

Great and striking was the contrast between the prophet on the one hand and the idolatrous Israelites on the other. They were in want, notwithstanding the extent of their country; they were writhing with vexation and misery, and their numbers, instead of being a mutual help and comfort, served only to make the common affliction more conspicuous and crushing. Day and night followed each other, only to tell them, like a succession of unwelcome witnesses, that there was no break in the gloom, no change in the wearying monotony of the drought. The air was burdened with vain supplications to their gods for a help which never arrived. Such was the state of the people of Israel; how different the lot of the prophet! He was alone, yet in peace. The drought and famine surrounded but did not harm him, and rather than that he should suffer, twice a day did a miracle take place for his sake, with the regularity of a natural law, for God never abandons those who faithfully and promptly obey His commands.

The prophet had no sooner done one task, that of delivering his perilous message, than he was called to another of a totally different kind, and by which his patience and trust were put to no ordinary trial. Instead of one duty being immediately followed after its fulfilment by a balmy repose or reward, it is quickly succeeded by another. We perform, for example, some unmistakable act of self-denying charity to others, and instead of being immediately recompensed by an accession of interior joy or exterior prosperity, we fall into unexpected difficulties, both spiritual and temporal. We are converts, perhaps, who have embraced the true Faith at a great loss of much that formed an integral part of our former happiness; we lose friends, are calumniated and suffer various discomforts; it is a crisis in which extra sunlight is counted upon as a certainty, and almost claimed as a right. We may have it, but on the other hand, we may find ourselves soon after our entrance into the "city of peace" treading a path of peculiar loneliness. Some again, who have for a long time led sinful lives finally break with the past at the cost of struggles requiring much courage and mortification; and yet, before there has been time to rest after the exhaustion of the strife, new duties have to be encountered which demand fresh sacrifices.

In these and similar cases there will be no danger to us if we are well furnished with faith and the spirit of obedience. We know that "to them that love God all things work unto good." (Rom. 8:28) In the midst of our trials we shall be certain to find, like Elias, a secure cave into which no real evil can enter. In a "barren and dry land" our Carith of refreshment will be near.

God may often send us into the midst of unforeseen circumstances, distasteful to our inclinations; circumstances to the eye unillumined by faith, ominously suggestive of evil rather than good. These are but the salutary disguises of

The Drought

mercy, and we shall be constrained to exclaim: "Blessed be God for them all! We thought at first, in our timidity and ignorance, that they were birds of prey, coming to search us out and rob us of our peace; but soon we discovered that, like the dark-winged ravens of the prophet, they were precious, though mysterious, messengers, sent to us direct from our heavenly Father, for the support and consolation of our souls."

If God had not intended to employ Elias in carrying out other designs of His providence, the prophet might have remained in the same abode until the cessation of the drought; for, although the torrent of Carith dried up, as we are distinctly told, yet it was just as easy for the divine power to make it flow with perpetual water as it was to feed Elias every morning and evening, by means of the miraculous ravens.

The servant of God was, however, called to another work.

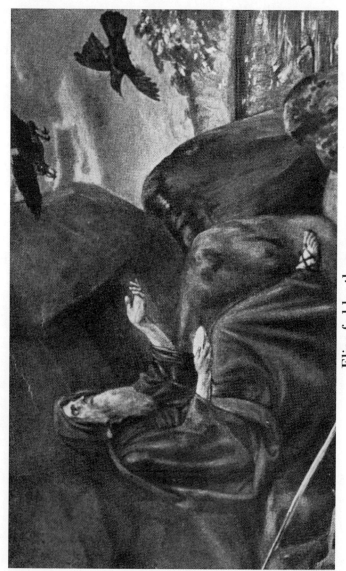

Elias fed by the ravens

Chapter Three
Sarephta

Surge, et vade in Sarephta Sidoniorum, et manebis ibi; praecepi enim ibi mulieri viduae ut pascat te.

"Arise, and go to Sarephta of the Sidonians, and dwell there: for I have commanded a widow woman there to feed thee."
— 3 Kings 17: 9

The actions and even the lives of persons differing widely in character and circumstances are sometimes linked together in a wonderful way.

At Carith, Elias was entirely alone. He was as a lamp of the sanctuary burning in the deep stillness of midnight, without the presence of any witness. He is now to step forth from his solitude, and to become the chosen instrument for drawing out from the soul of another, and manifesting to the world, a signal act of heroic faith. He, a Jew, is to bring to light, the unlooked-for spectacle of a pious Gentile, at the identical time when the Israelites were in full and shameless rebellion against the God of Abraham, of Isaac, and of Jacob. Elias is ordered by the "word of the Lord" to go to Sarephta, a place situated on the coast of the Mediterranean, not far from the famous city of Sidon. He immediately obeys, and just as he is on the point of entering the gate of Sarephta, he perceives a certain woman stooping down to gather sticks. This circumstance does not at first seem likely to be pregnant with any very remarkable issue. What is there particularly striking in the fact of a woman engaged in collecting a few bits of wood? This apparently very ordinary event leads, however, to something very extraordinary. Just as sometimes a small and mean looking door opens unexpectedly into a costly interior, so this first meeting between the prophet and the humble stickgatherer

The Prophet of Carmel

leads to golden results. Who and what is she? She is a widow, and that fact alone tells its own tale of bereavement. But she is not childless. She has a son, and thus her cloud of sorrow has its streak of silver lining. Here, at least, she has some consolation. In that child she ever beholds the memory of her husband who is no more, the dead father lives again in the son, and the mother's affections, sorely torn by her loss, may be partially healed. Her boy shall be her daily thought and legitimate pride; and when her last hour shall come, those hands which she has so often caressingly held and guided in infancy shall close her eyes in peace.

Such might have been a true picture if the drought and famine had stayed their course, and not touched Sarephta; but the blight of the judgment is there also and the widow's home has not escaped its effects. The dearer her child the more harrowing to her are the privations which both of them are obliged to endure. Far and wide has she searched, in the hope of obtaining a renewed supply of food, sufficient at least to ward off absolute starvation. All is gone except a little flour and oil! With quivering heart she watches day by day her child's failing strength and hears his plaintive cry of hunger. At length, all expectation of aid from her neighbors, who were suffering like herself, being given up, she goes forth from her home to gather for the last time, as she believes, a few sticks, to make a fire on which to prepare the final meal. The prophet stops her with an urgent request: "Give me a little water in a vessel that I may drink." (3Kng. 17:10) He asks only for a little water, enough to relieve the pain of thirst, for he who has brought the drought upon the land knows that it is scarce. Rare as it is, she is willing to procure it for him without hesitation or delay. Elias,

28

perceiving her charity, proceeds to try it more deeply by a harder test. "When she was going to fetch it, he called after her saying, bring me also, I beseech thee, a morsel of bread in thy hand." (3Kng. 5:11) In the agony of her distress she must have been sorely tempted to complain of the apparent heartlessness of this second appeal. Was it not enough to be asked for water, without having another most unreasonable demand made upon her, as if by an ironical afterthought, just as she was starting to fulfill the first? Who was this unknown stranger, this exacting Israelite? Was he mocking her because she was miserable and a Gentile? If such a thought passed through her mind, it had no influence upon her heart, for this was her answer: "As the Lord liveth, I have no bread, but only a handful of meal in a pot, and a little oil in a cruse; behold, I am gathering two sticks, that I may go in and dress it for me and my son, that we may eat it and die." (3Kng. 5:12)

"That we may eat it and die!" What a depth of woe and tenderness is revealed in these few words! The last morsel shall be shared with her child, and this is to be their parting meal. As they have lived together in one country, in one city, in one home, so they have resolved to expire together. Out of the same gate the same mourners shall bear the famished mother and her son, and in one grave shall be buried both their sorrows and their remains. Such were her despondent thoughts; but now a strange prodigy is on the point of taking place — a prodigy in which she is about to play an important part, and yet of whose probability not a gleam had ever passed through her imagination.

"Elias said to her, Fear not, but go and do as thou hast said; but first make for me of the same meal a little hearth-cake, and bring it to me, and after, make for thyself and

The Prophet of Carmel

thy son. For thus saith the Lord, the God of Israel: The pot of meal shall not waste, nor the cruse of oil be diminished until the day wherein the Lord will give rain upon the face of the earth." (3Kng. 17:13,14) As this desolate widow listened to these words, a terrible struggle must have passed through her heart. There was only a morsel for herself and her son at the most. Was she to share it with another? Was she to give it to him first? To one, moreover, who was not of her own kindred or nation? True, he promised that if she made this venture, the flour and oil should not decrease, but what proof had she that a miracle would be wrought for her? Why should the God of Israel violate the laws of nature for a Gentile? Elias had made a promise, but where was the seal of his words? What previous visible miracle had he wrought in order to justify her in believing that he could work another wonder? Rapidly as lightning these thoughts must have passed through her mind. She looked at the prophet, and she thought of her son. For a moment there was a pause, the mother's soul rocked to and fro between doubt and faith, between despair and hope. Then, by the mighty power of grace, it leaped at a bound over all difficulties. At the very brink of the grave, she believed in the prophet; and relying on the veracity of his words, threw, like another widow, her mite, with a generous boldness, into that treasury of the providence of God which ever gives back a thousandfold more than it receives. Faith wrestled with sight, and conquered. Divine charity rose intrepidly above the strongest of earthly affections. Piety towards God and His servant changed the timid mother into the fearless disciple. "She went and did according to the word of Elias." (3Kng. 5:15) Nor was she disappointed; she had boldly placed her trembling feet upon the hitherto untried

30

ground of the prophet's promise, and she found it to be solid rock. There was hunger in many houses, but into her dwelling it never entered, for a constant miracle was her unfailing support, her wonder and her joy. "There were many widows in Israel" and elsewhere; but in regard to her alone is it said, that "the pot of meal wasted not, and the cruse of oil was not diminished, according to the word of the Lord which He spoke in the hand of Elias." (Lk. 4:25 - 3Kng 17:16)

The widow of Sarephta! She went out of the gates on an errand of motherly devotion, and she met that great prophet of the Lord whom, for more than three years, the earth and heavens obeyed. She made, with intense humility, a mighty act of faith, and her immediate reward was a daily miracle in her home, life prolonged for herself and her child in a land of famine; whilst, as if to increase her unexpected happiness, Elias himself, instead of disappearing, like some brilliant meteor, as suddenly as he came, took up his abode with her as a guest, and shared with her that same simple yet miraculous meal which his own word had promised and produced.

To any bystanders who may have happened to see her on that occasion when she was gathering her two sticks for a little fire, by which to make her last meal, how unimportant she must have appeared! Yet her history, brief as it is, will be told over the whole globe until the hour strikes for the dissolution of the world. The famous city of Sidon could, in the days of its commercial glory, boast of many merchant princes, who were probably as much distinguished for their liberality as for their wealth. The renown of Sidon, however, is now only a tradition; scarcely a ruin of the ancient city remains to mark the burial spot of its former splendor. But the widow of

The Prophet of Carmel

Sarephta, though her name be unrecorded, is immortalized forever in the pages of revelation and in the memory of the faithful. Let us learn from her a lesson of humble trust, of venturesome self-sacrifice and of unstinting liberality. We may not have much to give to Almighty God. Our whole life would be little as an offering, even if we were to devote to His service all our substance, talents, time, opportunities, actions, words and thoughts; these are, at most, only as the morsel of bread and the single cruse of oil. Nevertheless, whatever we may be able to offer, let us give it to the glory of God, give it in faith, give it at a cost, give it without grudging or repenting, give it from that motive of divine love which transfigures the meanest things into grandeur, then we, like the widow, shall assuredly obtain an abundant reward.

Our little mite shall be multiplied a thousandfold; we shall have in this valley of tears a bread of fortitude and an oil of joy, which will not "waste" nor be "diminished," although all earthly supports and pleasures may vanish, as the dew and the rain disappeared from the land smitten by Elias.

But great as is the recompense even now, it is "not worthy to be compared with the glory to come." (Rom. 8:18)

The holiest amongst men live, whilst in this land of exile, only a rudimentary life. They are "babes" and not "perfect men." They can enjoy only a very partial participation of God. They "stand behind the wall looking through the windows, looking through the lattices," (Cant.2:9) seeing "through a glass in a dark manner;" (1Cor. 13:12) but as yet they have not entered into the paradise of their Beloved, "to feed in the gardens and to gather lilies." They do indeed possess a really supernatural nourishment in the "grace and truth" of the kingdom of Christ,

Sarephta

but even this is given that they "may eat and die" — that they may die in the peace of the just, in the sure hope of a glorious resurrection, "die in the Lord," by a death which is but the starting point, the nativity of a deathless life. Still, as long as they are "in the body," it must be confessed with St. Bernard, "that even their highest spiritual food, if contrasted with what is in store for them above, is only the husk of the grain." (In Solemn. Omn.Ss.n.3) They are in Sarephta, not in Zion. Hereafter they shall enjoy "that marrow of the wheat, that essential richness of corn, with which the holy city of Jerusalem is fed to satiety." Hereafter they shall experience the full meaning of the words of our Lord when He said: "I dispose to you, as My Father has disposed to Me, a kingdom, that you may eat and drink at My table in My kingdom." (Lk. 22:29,30)

The Vision on Carmel

Chapter Four
Mourning and Joy

Quid mihi et tibi, vir Dei? Ingressus es ad me ut . . . interficeres filium meum?

"What have I to do with thee, thou man of God? Art thou come to
me ... that thou shouldst kill my son?"
— 3 Kings 17:18

Let us transport ourselves to the house at Sarephta,
where the widow and her child, having been saved by the
word of Elias from perishing, now vie with each other in
expressions of mutual gratitude and trust. Day by day the
miracle of the perpetuation of the flour and oil continues.
In a land of sadness there is one little corner where a lamp
of joy is ever burning. The widow's lonely dwelling is a
spot unfailingly green in the center of a desert. Famine
comes to the very threshold, and there stops; as if being
spellbound by an invisible power, it dared not advance a
single step within the charmed enclosure. The prophet,
the widow and her son form a kind of "holy family" in a
place that was lying under a malediction. Who could have
imagined that so sweet a calm was about to be broken, and
that the hand of God would soon and unexpectedly cast a
dark shadow upon the common joy!

The child had escaped death from hunger, but the mother's heart was soon to be pierced by another calamity.

In the midst of sufficiency her son "fell sick, and the sickness was very grievous." (3Kng. 17:17) We can picture to
ourselves what this implied. Day by day the flour lasted
and the oil failed not; but day by day the strength of her
boy became less; his cheeks waxed paler and paler; his
eyes lost that winning radiance which is the usual charm of
health and youth; and the elastic spring and spontaneous

The Prophet of Carmel

activity of his limbs were changed into unwonted alternations of involuntary restlessness and unnatural languor.
This alteration, occurring without any obvious cause, suggested consequences which, however painful to contemplate, could not be dismissed, without deliberate self-
deception, from a mother's mind.

Was it possible that life could be ebbing, whilst the
mighty prophet was actually dwelling under the same roof
with the widow and her son? Was the grave, after all, to
gain the victory, prematurely, as it always seems in the
case of those whose years are as yet only in the bud? Had
famine, baffled as it had hitherto been in securing its prey,
found an avenger of its defeat in disease?

The trial was, indeed, very hard for that widowed mother to bear. Fear and hope came and went, the images
called up by each mingling for a time confusedly with each
other, until by degrees the former prevailed. Again and
again that mother anxiously caressed her child, as if she
believed that love could stay the advance of a malady. At
last the dreaded moment came when there was no
response, however feeble, to her signs of affection. She
fixed upon him a look so tender in its concentration of sadness, affection and breathless alarm that her whole soul
seemed to have been poured out in that one gaze, but no
glance of recognition came back. She called him by the
familiar name; he did not hear, for the spirit had fled, and
his form lay still and lifeless in her arms.

The agony of a great woe is sometimes almost a madness.
The soul, goaded on by its present real misery and by the
additional disturbing forces of an overexcited imagination,
does not stop to reason impartially, but plunges about
blindly. How strangely do persons to whom the above
description applies speak and act. How inconsistent they

are, how unlike their real selves. How singularly will some idea, of which they would in other circumstances take little notice, assume large proportions, seize hold of and dominate their minds! Such a crisis, not infrequently, does a wholesome work to the sufferer; it is a kind of mental earthquake, trying the soundness or weakness of foundations, and exposing to the light of day things which were not improving the atmosphere of the soul by being covered up.

Such was the conduct of the widow of Sarephta. The death of her child had shaken her soul severely. In her mind it became invested with a significant meaning not apparent to a stranger. Nor was the helpless form of her child the only object which disquieted her. From the child her eyes turned to the prophet. Elias was to her no longer the kind friend and welcome guest; he seemed to be like the silent finger of God, pointing at, following and probing her to the quick. She quailed under the scorching light of his presence, whilst she was stung by her loss into bitter recrimination. Out of those ruins of hope and joy which the death of her child had made, conscience rose up, as the spirit of Samuel before the panic-stricken Saul in the cave at Endor, and all her sins issuing forth from the recesses of memory, as from a tomb long closed and now suddenly burst open, took shape, and passed like so many condemning witnesses before her. Alarmed by this internal vision, she thought that Elias had come to smite her with the sword of the Lord and said: "What have I to do with thee, thou man of God? Art thou come to me, that my iniquities should be remembered, and that thou shouldst kill my son?" (3Kng. 17:18) In her distraction, she does not complain that he did not use his great power to prevent her son from dying, but she implies by her question that he had been the active cause of her loss. "Art thou come. . . that thou shouldst kill my son?" Disconsolate mother! Had she reflected for a moment, she would have perceived that nothing was so improbable as that he, who had saved her, her son, and her whole "house" (3Kng. 5:15) (for others were dependent upon her) from famine, and by virtue of whose promise the flour and oil remained still unexhausted, should intentionally have slain her son.

A charge so unjust and rash might have made an ordinary man indignant. See how Elias meets it. This prophet, so stern in his fiery zeal for God, is meekness itself; not one syllable of reproach escapes from his lips. He feels that before such a grief as that of the bereaved mother he must be silent. He does not defend himself, nor does he lose time in useless regrets. For true charity is prompt to action, as well as sympathetic; its tears do not end in themselves, but flow into a practical channel. "Give me thy son," Elias exclaims, and taking the dead child from the mother's arms, where she was still pressing it to her bosom as if that could give it back life, and carrying it up to his chamber, he lays it "upon his own bed." The deep stillness of that chamber is now broken by the voice of Elias, saying: "O Lord, hast Thou afflicted also the widow (with whom I am after a sort maintained), so as to slay her son?" (3Kng. 5:20) No answer comes; death still reigns supreme. Then Elias, finding that this question, which was a prayer in spirit, if not in form, produced no effect, "stretched and measured himself upon the child three times, and cried and said: O Lord my God, let the soul of this child, I beseech Thee, return into his body." (3Kng. 5:21) Words alone even from Elias are not sufficient to work a change. He must bow down his body, as well as lift up his heart in prayer. Not once only, nor twice, but three times, contracting himself, he must touch and breathe into the lips of the child with that same mouth which had prophesied against Achab, and received the food brought to him miraculously by the ravens at the cave near the brook of Carith. He must apply to the diminutive, motionless frame of a young child those hands so mighty for blessing or anathema, and those feet which were often wearied by their journeyings in the service of God. Strength must humbly adapt itself to weakness; freedom must link itself with captivity; and life must embrace death. The ambassador of heaven must lower himself to an equality with the offspring of a Gentile woman, in order that the desired miracle may be wrought. After taking up the child into his arms, after "strong crying," after a triple prostration of his own body over the corpse, face to face, limb to limb, heart to heart, then, and it was not until then, as we are told, that "the Lord heard the voice of Elias, and the soul of the child returned and he revived." (3Kng. 17:22)

After obtaining from God this great miracle — it was the first resurrection that had been seen since death had entered the world — Elias showed as much lowliness and self-forgetfulness as if he had done nothing unusual. He did not summon the widow to come up to him and to take the child back herself. This prophet, who had neither wife nor child, and who has been ever considered to have been the typical exemplar under the Old Dispensation of future solitaries and ascetics under the New, carried beneath all his exterior roughness the heart of the tenderest of fathers. He took the dead child into his arms and, when it was restored to life, hastened with thoughtful eagerness to lay him quickly yet gently upon his mother's bosom. She must receive him direct from the jealous guardianship of Elias' own hands, shining radiantly with the delight which must have followed the sense of new vitality. "He delivered him to his mother." How lowly were his words! Not one syllable did he utter about himself, not one word about his prostrations and prayers. He seemed to forget all but the mother's restored happiness, and instead of saying, "Behold what I have done for thee," exclaimed only, "Behold, thy son liveth." (3Kng. 5:24) What a change for her, and how different was now her language about Elias! A little while ago it was, "What have I to do with thee, thou man of God? Art thou come to me, that my iniquities should be remembered, and that thou shouldst kill my son?" But when she saw and felt her child fresh from the prophet's care, no longer dead, but smiling into her tearful eyes, she made no immediate allusion to her son or to her own delight, but as if borne along by the strong current of an overwhelming supernatural conviction, she burst forth into this profession of faith: "Now I know that thou art a man of God, and the word of the Lord in thy mouth is true." (3Kng. 5:25)

A great mystery was symbolized by the conduct of the prophet in taking the corpse of the widow's child into his arms, laying it upon his own bed, and prostrating himself over it three times. The lifeless child represented man after the fall; man whose soul withered and became corpse-like when the divine breath of grace departed; man with his reason dimmed so that it could not discern clearly the truth about himself and God; man with his conscience benumbed so that it could not feel sensitive, as it ought to have done, to the slightest indications of right and wrong; man with his will so sluggish and drugged as to sink easily under evil. Such was man after the fall, and such would he have remained for ever if an Elias far mightier than the Thesbite had not come forth from that unspeakably sublime solitude, the hidden depths of infinite love, to raise him up from his otherwise irreparable ruin. Who is it that stooped down from on high and entered the narrow chamber of this sin-stricken world of ours, in order to take off its malediction, to bring light into its darkness, and to open within its fatal labyrinth a sure and clear path to the heaven from which He descended? Who is it that contracted His infinity, as it were, to a point, in order to unite it with the smallness of our finite nature? Who is it that, in order to accomplish a union so humiliating to Himself, and so exalting for us, chose to be "made of a woman," so that He who had neither beginning nor end became for us a little child? Who is it that abased Himself for our sakes not for a short time only or exteriorly, as Elias narrowed his form to that of the widow's son, but assumed a second and created nature unspeakably inferior to the first, and yet eternally inseparable from it? Who is it that gave not only His breath, like Elias, but even His life for the dead? Who is it that, not content with offering up that life once and on one spot, dies mystically every day and in every land? Who is it that not only bestows upon us, without any previous merit of our own, many gifts distinct from Himself, but feeds us with Himself, and by a union as incomprehensible as it is real, entering into and pervading our souls and bodies with His own Soul, Body and Divinity, thus makes man become one with God? According to His own words: "He that eateth My flesh and drinketh My blood abideth in Me, and I in him." (Jn. 6:57)

We recognize Him well and in a moment. It is the Son of God, the King of kings. He it is who, emptying Himself of His glory, took our nature, and weaving it together with

The Prophet of Carmel

the Godhead, yet without "confusion of substance," in the womb of Mary, thus "laid it upon his own bed." In that virginal chamber the first prostration of the Elias of redemption took place, for there was first experienced the quickening touch of dead humanity by the Life of the world. The second "measuring" of Himself so as to fit the proportions of our littleness was accomplished when He condescended to be born in the poor manger at Bethlehem; and the third, when He extended His nailed hands and feet upon the cross. The prophet, when he "stretched himself upon the child," only assumed by that attitude the semblance of death, but Jesus Christ died no figurative death, He "yielded up the ghost." (Mt. 27:50) He "became obedient unto death, even the death of the cross."Phil. 2:8) "I lay down My life for my sheep," are His own words. (Jn. 10:15) He died, moreover, not for the Jew nor the Gentile only, but "for all," (2Cor. 5:15) not for the righteous only, but "for the ungodly." (Rom. 5:6) Nor did Christ die that we might obtain merely a temporal resurrection, such as took place at Sarephta. The life which the prophet restored was the same in kind as that which had animated the child, earthly and transient. It came back already sentenced to again depart; whereas "Christ died for us that we may live together with Him." (1Thes. 5:10) Who has said, "Behold, I am living for ever and ever." (Apoc. 2:18) "This is the promise," writes St. John, "that He promised us life everlasting." (1Jn. 2:25)

Let us note the unflagging perseverance of Elias when seeking to obtain for others a special mercy from God. Had he become impatient, had he prayed only with the force of a momentary impulse of zeal and pity, had he made no fresh efforts beyond prayer, the chain of death would have remained unloosed. But he left no means of success untried. He threw his whole heart into the work and, therefore, "the Lord heard the voice of Elias, and the soul of the child returned to him, and he revived." How many sons and daughters of another and spiritual mother are lost to her, without any resurrection, owing to the want of fervor and perseverance on our part. They have been once born supernaturally through the sacrament of regeneration; they have been fed upon infallible truth, and fenced from evil by tender and wise discipline. Nevertheless, having yielded to the fascination of some mortal sin, they have died upon their mother's bosom without recovery. We allude to the Church of God, and to those who, without being apostates from the faith or visibly cut off by ecclesiastical censure from membership with her, have perished through their iniquity whilst still bearing the name of her children. She is a mother without an equal or a rival. She is a mother of an only son, for she yearns lovingly over each of her offspring as though she possessed but one; and all her children form together "one body." She is a widow also, because her divine Bridegroom is still absent, and she is desolate till He returns. True it is that there is joy ever mingled with her tears, for if some of her children never awake from spiritual death, yet many are saved. And as they revive and are delivered to her arms again, the angels seem to whisper to her as they bend exultingly over each, "Behold, thy son liveth!" Still the question forces itself upon us with relentless intensity: why are there not more spiritual resurrections? Why is the funeral of the sinner's body preceded so often by one far more sad and awful, the burial of the sinner's soul? One reason amongst others is this: we have not the spirit of

The Prophet of Carmel

Elias; we have not prayed for sinners with his fervor; we have not lowered ourselves in humility and gentle charity to their many infirmities. We have not had his patience and have, therefore, ceased our endeavors before the time of the Lord had come. We have not been always earnest ourselves, and consequently could not warm others with our own glow. We have not brooded over them with strong longings for their salvation, with words of pleading, and the quickening force of a consistent life. We, by our individual tepidity, lessen the joy of our Lord and of the holy angels and of the Church, inasmuch as, through our neglect, so many souls remain in perpetual death who might otherwise have been dwellers forever in the city of life.

Chapter Five
The Message of Mercy

Factum est verbum Domini ad Eliam . . . dicens: Vade, et ostende te Achab, ut dem pluviam super faciem terrae.

"...the word of the Lord came to Elias . . . saying: Go and show thyself to Achab, that I may give rain upon the face of the earth.
— 3 Kings 18:1

Between the first meeting of Elias with King Achab and the period to which we are now conducted by the sacred narrative, there had been abundant time for salutary reflections and repentance. The king's heart, however, like that of Pharaoh, grew only more stubborn in its evil perversity. The blows that should have shaken his resolution and made him bend under chastisement, lashed him into a fiercer and more defiant rebellion; his spirit glowed in the furnace to a red heat without melting. Two desires possessed him: the longing to battle successfully with the increasing force of the divine punishment, and to slay the prophet.

"There was a grievous famine in Samaria," and the cattle were evidently dying in great numbers, for the king, almost in despair, summoned "Abdias, the governor of his house," and determined to go with him and search far and near for water. (3Kng. 18:2) Abdias was a man who, in the idolatrous court of Achab, was faithful to God, and had hidden a hundred of His prophets "by fifty and fifty, in caves, and fed them with bread and water." Achab said to Abdias: "Go into the land, unto all the fountains of waters, and into all valleys, to see if we can find grass, and save the horses and mules, that the beasts may not utterly perish. And they divided the countries between them, that they might go round about them. Achab went one way, and

45

The Prophet of Carmel

Abdias another way by himself." (3Kng. 5:4-6) If we had known nothing of the cause of this famine, there would have been something most touching and almost sublime in that lonely melancholy search by the king and his minister for food to save the lives of the languishing cattle. As it was, the king only proved that he was no less hardened after three years of bitter experience of the anger of God, than he was before that anger had become a reality. He had learned no lesson of wisdom, and admitted no guilt. In Elias he saw nothing but a tormentor and a foe. With a singular fatuity he imagined, probably, that the prophet had some kind of magical power over the elements, and that if he could only be swept out of this world and extinguished, the sorcery would be dissolved, and the rain would again fall from the heavens. Achab, therefore, sought for the prophet with the eagerness of a hunter after his prey, so that, as Abdias said to Elias, when he met him: "There is no nation or kingdom whither my lord hath not sent to seek thee; and when all answered, "he is not here," he took an oath of every kingdom and nation because thou wast not found." (3Kng.18:10)

What a contrast is thus brought before our mind! Achab caring so much for his horses and mules that he searches far and near for a little grass to keep them from dying, and on the other hand making "every nation and kingdom" within his royal jurisdiction swear a solemn oath that they had not found Elias, whom he was yearning to slay! He counts the life of his dumb irrational animals to be more precious than that of the Lord's own prophet, a striking example of the incredible ignorance and the utter anarchy of judgment to which any soul is liable, into which the darkness of some blinding passion has been allowed to enter and reign. If the king is seeking for Elias

46

The Message of Mercy

in order to pour upon him the full torrent of his
vengeance, the prophet is seeking for the king with a far
different object. The one thirsts for blood, the other is
coming with a message of mercy. He who is pursued as a
victim hastens to disarm his persecutor by an offer of
kindness. How does this, we may ask, come to pass? What
has softened the anger of the prophet? What has induced
him to bear tidings of peace in reply to a deadly challenge? It is not the prophet who has changed; it is the
prophet's Master who is willing to forget even the past
ingratitude and present audacity of Achab if he will only
repent. How wonderful is the compassion of God! He
seems to act as though He Himself felt the very pain
caused by His own necessary justice. "If He hath cast off,
He will also have mercy according to the multitude of His
mercies, for He hath not willingly afflicted nor cast off the
children of men." (Lam. 2:32) "The Lord," we are told,
"came to Elias in the third year, saying: Go and show thyself to Achab, that I may give rain upon the face of the
earth." (3Kng. 18:1) Elias was a man so full of zeal that
he appears to have had no thoughts of relaxing the
drought which he had brought upon the land, until he
received the above command from his Lord. Truly, as
David said, "It is better to fall into the hands of the Lord,
for His mercies are many, than into the hands of men."
(2Kng. 24:15) God was full of compassion for the suffering Israelites and for Achab, and, therefore, He arranged
for Elias to meet Achab in order to give another opportunity of conversion to this misguided king. God wished the
rain to fall as a miraculous and merciful answer to Achab's
repentance, if it should take place; but at the same time He
was desirous that in each of these events the finger of His
prophet should be an important element. No language

47

The Prophet of Carmel

could show more clearly the intention of God to give personal honor to Elias, to bring him forward into an eminent position, to encircle him with a special authority and dignity, than these words: "Go and show thyself to Achab, that I may give rain upon the face of the earth." God was the Creator of the heavens and the earth, yet such is His marvelous condescension, such His ineffably delicate recognition of the prophet's office, such His infinitely royal courtesy towards His own ambassador, that He speaks as if the hands of His omnipotence must remain bound until they are loosed by the intervention of His own servant. "Show thyself to Achab, that I may give rain upon the face of the earth."

When Elias and Achab meet, the first words come from the lips of the king; he does not wait to ascertain what may be the prophet's intention in seeking him. The very sight of Elias is the signal for an outburst of anger; the "venom of asps is under his lips," and it darts forth without a moment's pause.

When he had seen him, he said, "Art thou he that troubleth Israel?" (3Kng. 18:17) One would have imagined that the king, in the midst of so much terrible suffering, would have been too much depressed to salute Elias with a sarcastic and mocking question. One would have thought that there would have been at least some misgiving in his own mind even about the policy of this mode of address. It was no less undiplomatic than it was insulting. It was the outburst of a narrow-minded, self-sufficient fanaticism, rushing heedlessly like a wild animal upon the first figure that dares to cross its path. Achab does not consider for an instant the right or wrong of the case; he does not analyze the moral nature of the peace which has been disturbed; all that he knows, feels and cares about is the sim-

The Message of Mercy

ple fact that his Israel has been "troubled;" Israel the idolatrous, Israel the voluptuous, the Israel which is kin to,
and has been more or less fashioned by, his own carnal
nature and that of Jezabel. This is one leading idea which
possesses his imagination, and the other is that the sole
spoiler of this state of peace is the man called Elias, upon
whose form his eyes now indignantly rest. With his heart
set upon idolatry and sensuality, he looks at Elias through
a misleading atmosphere. He measures him by a false standard. He discerns no trace of his mission from God. He
passes without any notice all the signs of his miraculous
power, trampling heedlessly upon them, though they
grievously wound his feet, as incautious travelers are
sometimes pierced by the hidden thorns of the brake
through which they are journeying. The real and sacred
character of Elias is invisible to Achab; like his own
images, "he has ears, and hears not; eyes, and sees not."
All that is grand about the prophet, all that serves as a key
to his actions, all that inspires, moves and guides him, all
that gives him substance, color and prominence in the
world, natural and supernatural, is to Achab either shad-
owy and unintelligible, or entirely non-existent. His
dwarfed vision can only take within its petty range a single characteristic, and this he sees in one exaggerated
light, and written as it were, in large characters all over
the person of the prophet — "the troubler of Israel."

49

Chapter Six
Troubling Israel

Tunc es ille qui conturbas Israel?

"Art thou he that troublest Israel?"
— 3 Kings 18:s17

As we gaze in fancy upon these two facing each other, do we not recognize something more than two individuals coming into collision in a transitory manner, and then passing each on his own stage of personal life? Does Achab's question begin and end with himself, or does it find a significant echo in the minds of many of us? If we understand Achab rightly, we shall see that he, himself, is a representative man on one side, as is the prophet on the other. Achab embodies the spirit of evil, the spirit of the world, and Elias embodies the spirit of the divine will, and of eternal morality. When the two fairly meet, there must be a conflict, for concord between them is impossible. Mutual attack is the condition of their existence. The peace represented by Achab is war to the peace represented by Elias, and the peace of the prophet is war to Achab.

The king of Israel has no lack of successors in the world. Every one who tries to extract pleasure out of sin, every one whose comfort depends on some unholy combination of interests and circumstances, every one whose vices have acquired that tranquillity, spurious though it be, which accompanies any settled habit, must feel like Achab when the real truth is pressed upon his notice. There are sinners so thoroughly hardened that nothing can disturb them. "I appointed watchmen over you, saying, 'Hearken

51

ye to the sound of the trumpet;" and they said, "We will not hearken." (Jer. 6:17) But most persons have not arrived at that terrible state, and an Elias will start up occasionally before them in the shape of their own conscience, facing them with a quiet presence more subduing than audible words. It comes like an apparition in the hush of the night, or in the peculiar loneliness of a sickbed, or in the desolation of a sudden affliction, and then it is that they are troubled. Happy will they be if their restlessness ends in repentance. But how many are there who, although they will not consent to abolish the idols of their heart, yet even in spite of their own wishes, dare not altogether turn away from the internal monitor whom God has sent to speak to their souls. They refuse to reform that Israel within them which they have created by their own passions and self-love, and they cannot, at a word, bid conscience vanish from their sight, or be "a dumb dog." What is the result? A life cankered by instability, uneasiness and ineffectual attempts at an impossible compromise between good and evil; a life of disappointment, confusion and bitterness; a life in which at last the soul becomes so sore, so irritated, so weary with its daily struggles against the light, that it sometimes, in a kind of momentary paroxysm of unrest, almost wishes that it had never known anything about God, and had never come across the presence of His grace.

We meet with persons now and then upon whose countenances a strange cloud of dissatisfaction seems to be brooding. We cannot account for this shadow, because if judged only outwardly, they seem provided with all that would naturally constitute felicity. They have wealth, friends and reputation. Something, however, is evidently wrong. They show in various ways traces of morbid mischief going on within; they find fault with others without any just reason at all, or to an excess utterly disproportionate to the merits of the case; they are capricious in their emotions, sometimes being violent and spasmodic in their demonstrations of enjoyment, and at other times sullen and moody. There is a want in them of balance and uniformity of conduct. Without any visible reason, they are at issue with themselves, their neighbors and their surroundings. If we could thoroughly unveil their interior, how often should we find the secret of their seemingly complicated misery to be nothing more than this: they are Achabs in disguise. They have Baal images and groves in that hidden home of their hearts into which the outer world is not allowed to enter; and when the spirit of unrest is agitating them, it is a sign that their conscience is at that moment rising up to deliver its message, and as Elias troubled Achab, so whilst conscience stands facing the soul, there can be no peace.

Achab's question is highly suggestive. Just as a few drops of a particular chemical fluid will instantly produce a change in another liquid, and reveal to demonstration the existence in it of a poisonous element, probably unsuspected before, so the presence of Elias acted instantaneously as a test of Achab's heart. If Achab had held the same principles as the prophet, if his mind had been in harmony with the will of God, as expressed by and through him, then Elias would have been received with a welcome; he would have brought with him the fragrance of peace and joy. Achab, however, resented as an intolerable interference every protest of the prophet. He had his own notion of happiness, and he did not want it to be unmasked and broken up as a horrible imposture of crime and delusion. His ruling wish was to maintain things in Israel as they were and, therefore, anything which exacted a change was

The Prophet of Carmel

to him an evil against which all his interests rose up in battle array as at the sound of a trumpet.

Let us test ourselves by Achab's question; let it serve as
our own barometer. When the will of God comes before us,
and comes in such a shape that we cannot fulfill it without
undergoing some kind of inconvenience, perhaps amounting even to a considerable dislocation of our actual life
arrangements, such as a severance of long and close
attachments, or a loss of ease, or money, or influences
which we prize, how do we meet that summons from God?
What is our first impression? What is our dominant fear or
hope? From what standpoint do we contemplate the bearings and probable consequences of our obedience? If the
idea of duty flows into our mind like a full tide, and at once
takes its rightful possession of our will, and if other considerations, such as the difficulty of submission, and the various sacrifices involved in it, merely follow the train of the
main thought without displacing its position or diluting its
force, then we may fairly conclude that our heart is in a
right   condition. We perceive the obstacles and we contemplate the necessity of pain if we carry out our duty. But
these reflections do not form the ruling spirit of our souls.
Their murmuring is heard like that of the seawaves which
beat around a ship without affecting its navigation. The
voice which we follow is "Thy will be done." This is the
keynote to our conduct; other voices may distract and
annoy us, but they do not command our allegiance. This is
loyalty to God. On the other hand, if, when we are confronted by a religious duty, the one dominant question
which is asked and felt throughout our whole being is —
how will my temporal interests be affected by it? — will they
be interfered with; must they give way; is there no escape?
— then it is a clear sign that we are cast in Achab's mold;

Troubling Israel

not on so large and gross a scale, but in the same essential
type. The first consideration in such a case is self, our carnal, unmortified, unsanctified self. We have built our house
out of our own materials, in our own fashion, upon
wretched sand, and we protest violently against that breath
of the Lord which is going to sweep it off its foundation.
When St. Paul was preaching at Ephesus, the chief commo-
tion was raised and fanned by Demetrius, the leading
idolatrous silversmith of the place. The artificers who made
silver temples for Diana were alarmed by his appeal: "So
that not only this our craft is in danger to be set at naught,
but also the temple of great Diana shall be reputed for nothing!" (Acts 19:27) The craft was in danger; that was the
critical issue; the great Diana herself was treated as only a
secondary and subordinate consideration; the goddess
brought grist to the commercial mill, and that was enough;
and as the divine preaching of the Apostle was a revolution
against "the craft" and its gains, it thus bore upon its face
its own condemnation in the eyes of the pagan silversmiths
of Ephesus. How often do Christians act upon the same
degrading   principles. They know that they ought to "do
all to the glory of God," and yet if this glory does not, as it
seldom does, fit in with their own plans, they treat it as an
enemy. The very suggestion of it is annoying; it spoils the
craft; it is a troubler of Israel and, for the sake of quiet,
must be, if possible, cast out of their path.

Many instances of the antagonism between man's ways
and God's ways will have formed part of our own experience. There is one phase of it which is to be found occasionally, though not often, in Catholic families, where,
beneath the crust of a decorous religious exterior, there is
ever smouldering a strong worldly element, which only

The Prophet of Carmel

awaits a particular time and circumstance to develop into rebellious, volcanic activity.

Parents who do not "seek first the kingdom of God" in all their home arrangements are certain to have an inordinate attachment to their individual desires and domestic schemes. They build castles in the air for each of their children. They take delight in drawing ideal maps of their futures. Instead of regarding their sons and daughters as a most sacred trust from God, and endeavoring to discover in what way they can best train them so as to carry out His blessed will, they regard them all as so much property. They are family jewels, to be worn as ornaments of the common home, as long as possible, and then to be skillfully invested in some advantageous social speculation. As long as nothing interferes with these worldly prospects, there is harmony in the house, and any ordinary spectator would never imagine the possibility of a painful change. The Spirit of God, however, "breatheth where He will," and often, when utterly unexpected, enters this fold "like a thief in the night," and whispers to one of the lambs, "Hearken, O daughter, and see, and incline thy ear, and forget thy people and thy father's house." (Ps. 44:11) "Arise, make haste, My love, My dove, My beautiful one, and come." (Cant. 2:10) What is this divine breathing? It is the "Voice of the Beloved," the call of Jesus Christ, inviting His own elect to follow Him apart from the ordinary track of life to the higher mountain of a more perfect vocation. How is this wonderfully unmerited honor received by these worldly parents? Do they go down at once on their knees and thank God for His mercy? Do they, at least, try to rejoice even amidst the tears that must naturally flow at the thought of the separation which such a summons

56

entails? The intimation falls like an explosive shell amongst their selfish hopes. The will of God not having entered into their calculations, they are at first stunned, and then exasperated, by the discovery that, without their suggestion or sanction, it has carried their offspring into its sweet and glorious captivity.

For a son to become a priest or a monk, whom they had been sanguinely bringing up with a view to a brilliant and wealthy career, seems to them a kind of robbery of their just rights. The act is felt as a personal misfortune, and is not infrequently treated for a time as an instance of needlessly cruel opposition, the sublime inspiration of God being mistaken for filial ingratitude. In the case of a daughter's vocation to a religious state, the disquiet, the disappointment and the vexation are often still more intensified. What is the use of her costly accomplishments if they are never to be displayed? Her beauty and elegant manners might have drawn wealth, position and perhaps a title, into the family, but these two attractions are worthless if marriage is to be for ever renounced. What a waste to bury such a pearl in the sepulchre, however holy, of a cloister! Such is the miserable, one-sided, earthly reasoning of the world. All that is lovely, good, talented and attractive is to be jealously preserved for the use of ambition, show or, at best, for the increase of merely natural welfare and happiness, whilst the refuse of humanity may be thrown over into the garden of the Lord. If monasteries and convents would only be content to relieve households of useless encumbrances, if they would only provide an economical asylum for those of its members who are neither a credit, a comfort, nor a benefit to their relations, few complaints would be heard. But when they draw within their quiet walls those who have been ever

looked upon as the choicest flowers of the family, then
Achab's spirit breaks forth; then arise murmurings and
reproaches; then fathers are sullen or violent, and moth-
ers "will not be comforted;" then confessors, who were
formerly pronounced to be models of wisdom, lose all
their prestige if they confirm the vocation; then, unworthy and ingenious maneuvers are adopted for muffling, if
possible, the divine voice, and removing out of the way
everything that is likely to keep the supernatural flame
alive; then commences a series of domestic persecutions,
occasionally so severe as to make the candidate for a religious state almost a martyr before, a reluctant consent
having been given, the threshold of the old home is passed
and that of the new home entered.

Chapter Seven
Necessary Antagonism

. . . Non ego turbavi Israel, sed tu et domus patris tui,
qui dereliquistis mandata Domini . . .

". . . I have not troubled Israel, but thou and thy father's house who
have forsaken the commandments of the Lord . . ."
— 3 Kings 18:18

Achab's expressed hostility to Elias reminds us of another kind of antagonism, and one to which the Catholic Church is especially exposed. Achab wished to have his own way, to enjoy his own religious ideas, false as they were, without restraint. He began, probably, with the worship of the golden calves of Jeroboam; from this he proceeded to the worship of Baal and of Astaroth; and, no doubt, if another species of agreeable idolatry had been brought before his notice, he would have been quite ready to have adopted that also into his creed and practice. Elias, on the other hand, was the very type of inflexibility. He knew only one God, and he rejected with horror any deviation from His pure and simple law. Achab was elastic in his ideas of truth and morality, and open to new impressions; having once forsaken the true God, he yielded easily to the influence of Jezabel, and drifted with any current that flattered his passions and gratified his senses.

In this respect he is a representative of the extreme latitudinarian spirit of modern times. There is an avowed craving for unlimited change in religion as in other matters. The tendency is in favor of each man choosing that belief which seems to suit best his natural tastes. But however persons may differ amongst themselves as to the meaning of Christianity, there is one point upon which

The Prophet of Carmel

there is a sad unanimity of opinion — all have an intense dislike of the Catholic faith. Nor is this surprising. A message claiming to be divine and unalterable is a rebuke direct and irrevocable to the upholders of a system whose perfection consists in its capacity for variation. Absolute authority is galling to the desire of absolute freedom. Order is an intolerable yoke to the love of chaos. The exclusiveness of truth is tyranny in the eyes of those who are perpetually widening the stakes of their theological tabernacle so as to embrace any amount of contradictions. A strong fixed light is distressing to those whose ideal of mental satisfaction is to float dreamily on a misty ocean of opinion and sentiment, without knowing or caring to know whither they are really drifting. The assertion of Catholic dogmatic infallibility creates, and will always create, a strong sense of antipathy in the minds of all who prefer the idol of uncertainty, doubt, or what they call progress: a movement which, as understood by them, is only another name for change.

Besides the speculative Achabs of the day, who profess to act on scientific motives, there are others who become latitudinarians through mental sloth, rather than upon any distinct principle. They dislike definiteness in doctrine because they cannot bear the trouble of keeping their minds steadily up to any standard whatever; all exactness of statement demands from their languid intellects too much attention; precision means order, measure, proportion, and these qualities require a certain amount of watchfulness and steadiness of brain and will which is distasteful to them. They hate positive instruction, and, therefore, they have a natural antipathy to positive teachers. They love to lie down comfortably in the warm bed of their ignorance; vagueness is their pillow of rest, and they

Necessary Antagonism

do not wish it to be shaken, even for their own good. No wonder if such dreamy, lotus-eating individuals intensely dislike the Catholic Church, which speaks authoritatively because she has a mission to teach, and also because she sees clearly the meaning and bearings of her teaching. They want to be left alone, and she insists upon showing them the "narrow way" of truth, and urges them to walk in it, and in it alone. They want a soporific tranquillity, and she disturbs them by "crying aloud and sparing not." So enamoured are they of the tideless dead calm on which their minds float without moving, that if an angel were to stir the waters they would almost complain of such an interference. They resent anything like a cross examination, however friendly, on their religious ideas. If they were to see an apostle moving towards them to make a communication or put a few questions, they would be strongly tempted to look for a side path in order to escape from the interview.

It is frequently said by the enemies of the Catholic Church that she cannot be the Church of the Prince of Peace, because she is so constantly producing uneasiness, discord and agitation in the world. The mere fact of her not falling in quietly with the wishes of mankind in general, or with those of certain classes in particular, is interpreted to be a patent self-condemnation; as if the fact required only to be stated in order to carry judgment on its lips without further proof. The world takes for granted that its own wishes are to be the universal law, its own interests to be paramount over all others. It thinks that its own narrow circle is to embrace every other. It arrogantly claims possession of the whole field of thought, motive and action, and denounces any other system, society, or principle as a trespasser and usurper.

The Prophet of Carmel

Measuring itself by no standard except its own, seeing no farther than its particular horizon, filled with nothing but the huge shadow of its vain emptiness, it resents the presence of anything that seems like a rival, and still more of anything that claims to be its guide and master. It is not surprising, therefore, if it regards the Catholic Church with no common animosity, for the world and the Church are perpetually meeting, and they meet only for combat. If the Church would only just stand out of the way, if she would only be silent or ambiguous, if she would only consent to a bargain and a compromise, and split differences upon those points where the two are at issue, the world's dislike of the Church would not be so deep or lasting. But as Elias stood up and confronted Achab, man to man, eye to eye, voice to voice, so the Church confronts the world. There is no sphere in which a soul can sin or act righteously, no sphere in which even the body can be the instrument for evil or good, of Satan or of God, in which the Church does not claim to have the supreme sovereignty of direction.

The world, however, has no rights apart from or contradictory to the end for which God has created and redeemed man. Hence the world cannot have a creed, or gratify its passion, or amass and use wealth, or seek liberty, or govern politically, or educate its children in any way that shall be injurious to the attainment of the highest end of man, his sanctification and salvation, both of which converge into a farther end and perfection, the glory of God. This is a truth which the Church never forgets. It is her inspired instinct, her moving principle, her unchanging Credo. She stands ever before the world, with this sublime fire burning unquenchably within her, beholding her own self, end and means in the very same light which she casts upon the world. When, therefore, the world claims and tries to have a religious, a political, a philosophical or a commercial system entirely to itself; when, ignoring the revealed law of God, it hides, ostrich-like, its carnal eyes in the dust of this earth; when it switches immortality, heaven, hell and judgment, unceremoniously off its busy line, in order that its own train may pass on undisturbed, no wonder if it finds itself at war with the Church, if it has to hear a message that it hates, if it writhes under the only grasp that has the courage to arrest it.

As long as men act upon the principles of nature instead of grace, disowning the ineffaceable brand of the fall, and shutting their eyes and ears to the great fact and far-reaching consequences of the new kingdom of Jesus Christ, they must necessarily regard the Catholic Church as a foe to their peace, as an aggressive and dissolving element, as a provoking protester and witness against their maxims. What is more offensive to the worshipers of wealth than to have to deal, not with an abstract philosophy teaching the contempt of money for its own sake, but with a real living body, where mammon is attacked by example as well as by word? The mere sight of a voluntary Lazarus in the shape of a poor monk is gall and wormwood to the soul of the Dives of political economy. A system which considers individual property to be frequently a snare and clog to the soul, and hails its voluntary abnegation as a virtue, must derange sadly the fundamental ideas of that large class whose gods are "gold and silver." Do we not often find the Catholic Church condemned at once by Protestants because she is supposed not to encourage material progress as much as their own religion? The question really raised in their minds is not

The Prophet of Carmel

"Which is the true religion?" but "Which is likely to interfere least with the common desire for comfort, refinement,
luxury and increase of income"? Thus the preeminently
unearthly is judged by a standard preeminently earthly.
The commercial barometer is to interpret the state of the
spiritual heavens. The Stock Exchange is the grand final
court of appeal before which the "kingdom not of this
world" is to make its cringing bow, and justify its claims
on the souls of lost men, who have to be saved by the crucified Man of Sorrows!

If the Church troubled only the private "Israel" of a
few individuals, interfering exclusively with the favorite
idols of this or that person, without attempting more,
she would not meet with such widespread and bitter
opposition. The murmuring would be feeble and partial,
not strong and general. But there are upon the earth
various organizations, more or less extensive, of men,
laws and force, rulers and subjects, which are essential-
ly contradistinguished from the Church as being "kingdoms of this world." Now if the leading administrators
of these kingdoms do not recognize the divine primacy of
Christianity over all things secular; if their political
vision is so filled with Caesar that God is viewed only
through the image of Caesar, and His rights are treated
as null, or are suspended until they have been endorsed
by Caesar's signature; it is not difficult to foretell how
such rulers will feel and act towards the Church. Men of
this class become, often unconsciously, worshipers of the
government in which they play so important a part.
Fallible themselves, they nevertheless believe in the
infallibility of the State. Pygmalion-like they easily fall in
love with and adore that which they behold gradually
developing itself under the cunning skill of their own

hands. The State becomes their sacred fetish, and they passionately resist any free handling of it as an unnatural outrage. We cannot wonder, therefore, if the Church is often to such men an object of suspicion before she speaks, and of intense antagonism when she both speaks and acts; for the Church in her origin, her end and her means is far beyond and above all merely earthly empires. They can but extend over and act for this world. Their aim is external peace and welfare, and their methods of obtaining that end do not rise beyond this level; whereas the Church penetrates through the roof of this world into the next, and links the two together. She admits of no local barriers to her advance; she shares her jurisdiction with no other body, however large or powerful, being sole and sovereign in her own sphere. Her mission is universal in place and time. Her principles are divinely fixed for her, and therefore unchangeable, and presiding as she does over the souls of men, touching with her sceptre their reason and will, she has a conscience above all bribery and defiant of all compulsion. Being what she is, and even intensely conscious of her own identity and character, there are occasions when she would be faithless to herself and her King above if she did not pursue her path independently of the State, with its inferior, and too often immoral, principles, its carnal expedients, and its conveniences of the day. The Church is often accused of rebellious opposition to the State but she is never disloyal to the State unless the State is disloyal to God.

As long as governments are true to the object for which they exist, as long as they decree nothing contrary to justice, purity and religion, they will ever find the Church of Christ their strongest sustainer, instead of being either

The Prophet of Carmel

actively or passively arrayed against them. Had the Jews, who persecuted St. Paul, known the real spirit and end of the Mosaic law, they would never have charged the Apostle with being a "pestilent man and raising sedition."

If every conscientious refusal to be bound by the powers of this world in matters beyond their jurisdiction is in itself a crime, what then is the meaning of Christ's own prophecy about His disciples? Does He not solemnly warn them beforehand, and declare that they will be branded as rebels precisely on account of their allegiance to Him? "They will lay hands on you and persecute you; delivering you up to synagogues, and into prisons; dragging you before kings and governors for My sake." (Lk. 21:12) Does He blame them for this by anticipation? Quite the contrary: "it shall happen to you for a testimony." Their bonds will be a chain of glory for themselves, and a dishonor for their oppressors.

This prophecy of Christ, like all prophecies, was history in advance. We are not, therefore, astonished to find that fidelity to Christ has often brought, and will bring, upon the Church the obloquy of unfaithfulness to the State; but the fault lies with the State, and "the testimony" is with the Church.

The vital principle of the Church is to obey God and to carry out the universal mission of saving souls, as the ambassador of Jesus Christ upon earth. This is its one aim, its one law, its one discipline line, its one policy, its one wisdom, its one grand passion, its one duty. If unhappily it is summoned by politicians, be they monarchical or republican, to sacrifice its conscience to State expediency, its divine unity to the temporary centralization of governments, its inflexibility to the confused movements of the civil kaleidoscope, then it has no alternative but to exclaim with Peter and John of old: "If it be just in the sight of God to hear you rather than God, judge ye." And again, with Peter and the Apostles: "We ought to obey God rather than men." (Acts 4:19,29)

When Achab charged Elias with troubling Israel, the prophet did not content himself with merely denying the calumny. He hurled it back upon the king. He smote him with the edge of his own sword. He said: "I have not troubled Israel, but thou and thy father's house, who have forsaken the commandments of the Lord, and have followed Baalim." (3Kng.18:18)

The spirit of the prophet still lives, still speaks with fearless force in the person of the Catholic Church. "Ye Achabs of the present age," she says to her accusers, "you complain that I trouble your Israel in various ways; you say that I teach doctrines that are injurious to material progress and discouraging to liberty of thought; you charge me with meddling with questions out of my sphere, such as marriage, the rights of parents and children, education, the treatment of the poor and other matters that you consider exclusively secular; you condemn me as a political nuisance, as a social tyranny and, in a word, as a dangerous superstition, clogging with antiquated prejudices the nobly ambitious wheel of an advancing age. I, the Catholic Church, deny the justice of all these accusations, and affirm that upon your own heads recoils the bolt which you have launched against me. The 'Israel' for whose welfare both the State and the Church were created, is man himself; not man as a mere animal, not man with a destiny bounded by this earth, or the years of his short life, but man with a rational soul and an eternal future, man fallen, and for whose restoration and glorious elevation Christ has died. Citizenship here below has neither meaning nor rights, except so far as it is the training-school for that which is above.

"I alone have the great mission of leading this Israel, which is a 'pilgrim and a stranger on this earth, to a better, that is to say, a heavenly country." (Heb. 11:16) I alone, therefore, can give it a prosperity that will not pollute or fade away, a freedom which will not end in slavery, and a peace that will be neither the ominous herald of a storm nor a sign of death. The real troublers of the Israel of humanity are they who, by pandering to its unsanctified craving and divorcing it from religion, strike it a death-blow under the pretext of developing more fully its life."

Chapter Eight
Carmel

. . . *Usquequo claudicatis in duas partes. Si Dominus est Deus, sequimini eum . . .*

". . . How long halt ye between two sides? If the Lord be God follow Him . . ." — 3 Kings 18: 21

From the lonely conference between Elias and Achab, at which the prophet was arrogantly charged with being the disturber of Israel, the narrative now conducts us to another meeting of a very different character, a meeting as singular in its circumstances as it was important in its results. The spot where the memorable event took place which we are about to describe is of worldwide fame. It is a mountain whose form, rising out of the blue waters of an historic sea, and peering gracefully above craggy rocks, woody heights and undulating plains, gemmed with flowers of every hue, wields, even to this day, a kind of strange fascination over all who, having reverent faith, behold it either from the side of ocean or land.

The world possesses but one "Carmel by the sea." (Jer. 46:18) Carmel, a word which is still "a power" and, at whose sound, thoughts of loveliness (Isaias speaks of the "beauty of Carmel," 35: 2), grandeur and sanctity rise up into the mind, and follow instinctively in its train. Although the mountain itself may "languish, " (Nah. 4) and its "top be withered," (Amos 1:2) it has a fragrance and an immortality which shall never pass away. How can the name of Carmel die? Carmel, the ancient site of that "triumphant arch" near which Samuel foretold to the disobedient Saul the division of his kingdom" (1Kng. 15:12) the august scene of one, and probably two, of the most

69

The Prophet of Carmel

awe-inspiring deeds of Elias,[1] and the chosen retreat of himself and Eliseus; Carmel, set imperishably as a mystical jewel in the inspired poetry of Hebrew prophets; Carmel, far eclipsing, at a later epoch by the erection of its Christian altars, the sanctity of the old, and casting upon the entire Catholic Church a new splendor by the saintly brilliance of its monastic glory — a glory which, tracing back its natal rays to a no less august source than Elias himself, still lives; Carmel, the spiritual heirloom of a religious order, illustrious by the excellence of its deeds as well as by the continuity of its name! A peaceful silence usually prevailed within the solitudes of the mount. From its summit, the white tops of the houses in Jezrahel could be distinctly seen, gleaming in the sunlight through the clear distance, yet no disturbing hum from its streets could float so far. Little was heard upon Carmel except the sounds of the numerous wild birds and animals that haunted in comparative security its shady dells, or of the flocks that browsed upon the lower and more fertile slopes of the range, or of the wind, as sometimes it stole, moaning softly and plaintively, like a living creature in distress, amongst the caves and crags, and sometimes swept along, booming through the crashing trees with the roar of thunder. On a certain day, however, the wonted stillness of the mountain was broken by a sudden change. On every side was heard the tramp of a multitude, who were wending their way evidently towards some preconcerted spot. Their movement was quick, not from alarm, but from eager animation. On they went, a strange, motley army of men, women and even children, making the air a very Babel of loud and confused noise. On they went, winding

[1] Mount Carmel is commonly known among the modern Arabs as Jebel Mar-Elias, the Mountain of St. Elias. (Editor's note.)

Carmel

amidst vines and olives, and over gently swelling knolls, and through forest glades, until, regardless of the heat and toil which the scantiness of shade and water caused by the drought made exceptionally oppressive, they reached the end of the ascent. Amid the less orderly masses, yet distinctly separated from them, are two processions, marching in regular array, and easily distinguished by the conspicuous emblems of some superstitious worship, which they bear aloft with ostentatious pomp. Who are they that cast around them from time to time such glances of self-assured defiance? Who are they that so frantically clang their cymbals? Who are they that stop at short intervals, and with highpitched voices shout, and as they shout whirl swiftly round and round in the maddening dance, as if some unseen diabolic power were moving convulsively their pliant limbs? They are the prophets of Baal, four hundred and fifty in number; and in company with them are four hundred of the "prophets of the groves," the especial favorites of Queen Jezabel, who had the privilege of being daily guests at her table, and, in times of less scarcity than the present, reveled in its abundance and luxury.

On this occasion a king is present upon Mount Carmel. He is readily known by the splendor of his state robes, which he wears upon all unusually solemn days. Close to him are the chief officers of his court and the most distinguished warriors of his army. In spite, however, of all his magnificent exterior, there is within that breast, glittering with gold and jewels, a strong element of disquiet. Conflicting currents of feeling are passing through his heart, and his changing countenance betrays more perplexity and agitation than he wishes to avow. He is the prominent center of his own immediate circle, and behind

71

The Prophet of Carmel

and around him, stretching far into the distance, are the thickly clustering groups of his numerous subjects.

Why is it that the king, turning away from them, fixes his eye so anxiously upon a single spot, and watches so narrowly all the movements of a single individual! The king is Achab, and he has reason to be disturbed. Not far from his presence there is a man who, without any marks of royalty, without any retinue of courtiers to serve as a setting to himself, strikes every observer with the simple grandeur of his mien. Clad only in a mantle of sheepskin, he forms a strong contrast with the gorgeously dressed and effeminate priests of Baal. For a few moments he stands silently apart, as though the thought which was gathering up its forces within his breast were too mighty for manifestation. He is fronting thousands of hostile men yet, notwithstanding his conspicuous isolation, he knows that he is stronger than them all. How comes he there, and for what purpose? Strange to say, the proud king has, for once, acted as this man's herald, at his own request, and according to a previous mutual arrangement has summoned all the people to meet together, in order to come to the decision of a great question affecting their highest interests.

At their last interview, Elias had said to Achab: "Send now and gather unto me all Israel unto Mount Carmel, and the prophets of Baal four hundred and fifty, and the prophets of the groves four hundred, who eat at Jezabel's table." This was the request, and it was granted. "Achab sent to all the children of Israel, and gathered together the prophets unto Mount Carmel."(3Kng. 18:19,20) Elias has not been unfaithful to his own words. He had challenged the numerous priests of Baal and Astaroth to a public combat before the king and his subjects, a combat not of arms but of truth, a combat between the Living God and those counterfeit deities whom the apostate Israelites delighted to honor, and to whom they were sacrificing both their souls and their bodies; and now the hour for bringing his challenge to an issue is come, and he is here.

Elias addressed his first words directly to the people, not to the prophets. He speaks to the people in order to prepare their minds for the test which he is about to propose; for even a miracle might prove ineffectual unless their hearts were inclined to accept and appreciate its meaning. Like a skillful artist, he knows the advantage of painting upon a suitable canvas; he knows that the hard soil must be broken up if the seed is not to be dropped in vain; so he flashes a plain yet searching question before their minds. He appeals not to their imagination, but to their common sense, to the logic of their consciences. He does not attempt to conciliate them by any artificial rhetoric or evasive circumlocution, but strikes the target in its most central point. "Coming to all the people, he said, How long halt ye between two sides? If the Lord be God, follow Him; but if Baal be god, follow him." (3Kng.18:21) The listeners, who were probably expecting some elaborate argument, must have been startled to find themselves thus abruptly seized, as by a giant's grip, and made to face so closely the real issue that was before them. Let us observe both the wisdom and the delicate charity of Elias. He does not waste his time in appealing to the prophets of Baal and Astaroth, for he knew that they were strongly committed, on grounds of self-interest, to defend their position. Idolatry was their trade as well as their worship. Conviction of the truth would be to them equivalent to ruin; so he passes them by, conspicuously prominent as they were, and directs his question to those who were more hopeful subjects of persuasion. In this conduct Elias showed his wisdom, and his forbearance and

The Prophet of Carmel

charity are evidently discernible in the form of his appeal. Although he knew perfectly well that numbers of the people were entirely devoted to the worship of Baal and had no scruples about their iniquity, yet he also knew that there were others, who, not being so hardened, tried to make a compromise, and serve God and Baal at the same time. There were waverers and doubters among the people, and therefore, instead of denouncing the whole body with one sweeping anathema, he took for granted, with thoughtful tenderness, that the mass of them were sinning rather through sluggishness, indecision and instability than from a downright settled apostasy. He had good hopes of them, so he showed them their inconsistency, and tried to lead each man to convert himself by his own serious and rational reflections. He treated the matter as a question of time, and reproached them for their delay in not proceeding more quickly to a practical settlement. "Coming to all the people, he said, How long halt ye between two sides?"

The language of Elias, although addressed in this instance to the idolatrous Israelite, is far-reaching in the extent of its suggestiveness. The truth which it conveys is one which, though elementary, needs to be continually impressed on the minds of men. There are but "two sides," that of God and that of Baal. By Baal is to be understood everything which, not being on the side of God is, therefore, His enemy. "Thou shalt fear the Lord thy God and shalt serve Him only," (Deut. 6:13) is but a more ancient version of the same principle which our Lord proclaimed when He said: "No man can serve two masters." (Mt. 6:24) One of the most fatal delusions to which we are liable is the supposition that we need not commit ourselves to the service of God so exclusively as not to allow ourselves some degree of license in following our own tastes and passions, even though they are, when fairly judged, recognized to be inconsistent with the divine will. When Satan tempted Adam and Eve, he was too cunning to ask them, point blank, to renounce their Creator, he only proposed that they should disobey Him in one thing, insinuating that they might make a kind of compromise, and partly break and partly keep His law. He knew well, that if he could just persuade them to forget that they were the servants of God and of Him only, he would by that means plant in their hearts the radical principle of a universal rebellion. If the monarchy of God were limited, if it were a species of constitutional government in which the wheels are controlled by a series of checks and counterchecks, then such a scheme as Satan introduced might be conceivable. But since God is God and, therefore, the sole fountain of all rights and laws, any attempt to divide our allegiance with some other authority is really an attack upon God Himself. "Ye cannot serve God and mammon." This is an unalterable truth, but the devil is perpetually whispering to the souls of men: "You can! Try to make the most of both worlds; strike a bargain, so much of the spirit and so much of the flesh; so much of your own will and so much of God's will; so much of this world and so much of the next; take the philosophical, golden mean; be not great saints nor great sinners." How many are caught in this snare! How many waste their talents, time and energies in attempting the impossible! How many are eternally lost because they endeavor to go to heaven without absolutely serving God, or, as they foolishly suppose, without absolutely serving mammon! They are so infatuated as to hope that they can balance their souls in the air between heaven and earth as long as they like, without falling into the abyss below. In the world's politics we hear of truces, armistices, alternations of conduct, delicate adjustments of contrary interests, and noninterventions, simply because men are dealing with fellow men; but in questions which involve eternal principles and consequences there is only one side to be followed, only one Master and King to be obeyed with undoubting and unswerving allegiance. "Their heart is divided," said the prophet Osee, "now they shall perish." (Osee 2) They whom St. James describes as "double-minded men" are "inconstant in all their ways?" (Jam.1:8) they are religious by fits and starts, good one week and bad the next. They pray when they are in the humor, and cease praying when they are crossed and disappointed; they have no rule of life, but drift, like seaweed, backwards and forwards with the prevailing wind and tide. They spend days and whole years in passing and repassing between the camp of Satan and the camp of Christ, following nothing but their own changeable caprices. These may be said to be chronic halters between two sides, because, although they would deny that they ever really devoted themselves to the devil, yet they show no signs of being faithful and consistent servants of their Redeemer; and upon them will fall heavily the condemnation implied in His own solemn declaration: "He that is not with me is against me." (Lk. 11:23)

"How long do you halt between two sides?" This is a question full of meaning for those who, however well intentioned, are vainly endeavoring to have all the spiritual advantages of the Catholic Church without belonging to that one fold of Christ governed by the successor of Peter, which alone can claim their obedience by divine authority. Neither wishes, however strong, nor theories, however ingenious, nor historical views however boldly presented, nor eloquence in preaching, nor beauty in imitative ritualism, nor faith in the possession of sacramental powers, amounting almost to the sensation of infallibility, can create that which does not exist.

There are but "two sides" in the twentieth century, as there were in the first: the side of revelation, truth, grace, authority, unity and universality, represented and communicated by the Church of which Rome is the sole center; and the side of error, confusion, division and rebellion, represented and propagated by all bodies, no matter what be their names or origin, who are separated from the Apostolic See. The present is an age of mystifying scepticism of every kind; and not the least dangerous to Christians and dishonorable to Christ is that incredulity which treats the visible continuity of His kingdom as the temporary fact of a distant and irrecoverable past, and not as the divine reality of that momentous "now," in which our duties and our perils lie. There are men who say that since the disruption, East and West (the old landmarks) are gone, the old tests are obsolete and the old defenses against the mixture of falsehood with true doctrine, and of heretics with the orthodox in Christian communities, are no longer compatible with liberty and progress. They affirm that the sides are many and not two. Others, again, will not deny that perhaps there are two sides, but they declare that they feel unable to decide on leaving the one, in which birth, education or temporal convenience has placed them, for the other where it is clear that they will have to encounter much sacrifice. They consider the question, which is the side of God, to be a problem too hard for them to solve in so short and busy a life, and they hope not to be held seriously responsible for their ignorance. Others, again, are more industrious in pursuing the difficulty, but they follow it rather from the excitement of an intellectual chase than from the sole love

The Prophet of Carmel

of truth. They are ever halting between criticism and faith, or they are theological geologists trying to hold the balance between the Christianity which lies, comparatively speaking, fossilized in the vast strata of the works of the fathers, and that which is seen, heard and touched in the personality of the living Church, between the materials for composing an ecclesiastical essay, and a kingdom carrying on the administration of Christ upon the earth. There are also those who, chiefly attracted by their natural love of novelty, sentiment, religious diversion and dissipation — for there are such things — or with a shallow eclecticism, take a vague kind of pleasure in frequenting Catholic churches, gazing at Catholic ceremonies and even talking like interested amateurs of Catholic topics, without having the remotest intention of formally submitting to the Church itself. They are fond of going around the "enclosed garden" which Jesus Christ has planted in this sin-smitten world, admiring the beauty and the fragrance of its flowers. Now and then, in certain impressionable states of mind, they long to carry them off to their own dreary ground, where, if transplanted, they could never grow. In all this conduct there is nothing serious, and they never enter the paradise of the Church.

If we had the opportunity of speaking to any of those to whom these remarks apply, we should address to them the prophet's question: "How long do you halt between two sides?" "How long?" ask the ancient fathers, with one voice, eastern and western, who, though dead, still speak from their works. "How long?" cries the blood of the many martyrs who have sealed their testimony to the Catholic Faith by their death. "How long?" exclaim all who, from the highest bishop to the humblest layman, yearn for their salvation. "How long?" for the hours are flying quickly, and God is waiting for an answer.

There is one class of those who "halt between two sides," whose condition, whilst it is a heavy cross to themselves, also excites the deepest sympathy in the hearts of the faithful, and calls for their fervent prayers; those who, from the force of causes beyond their control, are innocently unable to embrace the truth because they cannot see their way into the Catholic Church with sufficient clearness to justify them in taking a step which demands the full and deliberate adhesion of the conscience. These are wandering sheep, who, if they could recognize the voice of Christ in the voice of the successor of Peter, would allow no earthly impediment to interfere with their obedience. Often they wither away in health and spirits through the wasting process of good will struggling ineffectually with those entanglements and pains of mental perplexity by which the inscrutable providence of God allows them to be tried. Though "seeking for light," they have "stumbled upon the dark mountains," (Jer. 13:16) but "there is nothing covered that shall not be revealed" (Mt. 10:26) in due time. If through no fault of theirs they approach the grave without entering the gates of unity, then in their last moments the scales will fall from their eyes; they will know the full truth, and the angels will recognize them as members of that "one fold"— of the Good Shepherd to which, through the grace of God, they had already belonged in soul though not in the visible body.*

That the question put by Elias to the Israelites had a strong effect is evident from the result. Instead of insulting him by defiance or interruption, they began to ponder quietly over his words, being also awed to a considerable degree by his earnest and authoritative manner. "The people did not answer him a word." It was the silence of respectful attention.

They were now ready to listen to his suggestion. "Elias said again to the people: I only remain a prophet of the Lord, but the prophets of Baal are four hundred and fifty men. Let two bullocks be given us, and let them choose one bullock for themselves, and cut it in pieces and lay it upon

* (Page 79) ßPublisher's Note: Father Garside is describing here a hypothetical case of what has to be a validly baptized Protestant who embraces the true Faith (and has perfect contrition for his sins) at the eleventh hour, i.e., on his deathbed. This is an extraordinary grace given by God for His own merciful reasons to one who has seemingly resisted grace his whole life long. No one who has heard and known the truth, as this man had, could be "innocently unable to embrace the truth," on account of some "mental perplexity." Saint Paul wrote that "charity rejoices in the truth," and without charity the soul is dead. The truth is never a cause of perplexity, error is the cause; the more obstinatly one clings to falsehood, the greater will be his inner perplexity. St. John writes that the Word of God "enlighteneth every man that cometh into this world." Our good author seems to be implying that there could be a man of good will who is simply unable to embrace the true religion because of some intellectual entanglement. The truth is that there is no obstacle that grace cannot overcome if a man cooperates with the work of the Spirit of Truth. Furthermore, as Pope Leo XIII taught in the encyclical *Divinum illud*, and Pope Plus XII reiterated in his encyclical *Mystici Corporis*, there is no "soul of the Church" in union with which one can be sanctified while refusing to join the "body." As with the physical body, the soul animates it and, being spiritual, is present wholly in every member and wholly in the whole body. The soul is what makes the living body an integral substance. It is the Holy Spirit that dwells within the living members of the Church, not as He does in the soul of Christ — that is without measure — but, as Pius XII taught, "according to the measure of the giving of Christ, out of Christ's own fullness." It is in this sense that Leo XIII did write these words: "Let it suffice to state this, that, as Christ is the Head of the Church, the Holy Spirit is her soul."

wood, but put no fire under it; and I will dress the other bullock, and lay it on wood, and put no fire under it. Call ye on the names of your gods, and I will call on the name of my Lord, and the God that shall answer by fire, let Him be God." The test was readily and universally accepted. "The people answering, said, A very good proposal." (3Kng. 18:22,24)

Elias, calm and confident, invites the idolatrous prophets to begin the ordeal. There is a latent irony in his courtesy: "Choose you one bullock and dress it first, because you are many." They shall have the precedence which their numbers, apart from any other consideration, would naturally seem to claim; the general attention being thus particularly directed to their superiority, in this respect to Elias, a fact which would, in case of a failure, tell against their cause with double effect.

The altar having been prepared, and the victim duly laid upon it, the idolatrous prophets commence their supplications. Far and near their many voices resound. Hour after hour passes by, and though in their fanatical excitement they leap over the altar, no answer comes except the mocking echo, repeated again and again, of their own words: "O Baal, hear us." The early morn grows into the full blaze of the midday sun, and the altar and the slain bullock remain unchanged. The continued absence of any supernatural sign that their offering was recognized by Baal must have been galling enough, but Elias intensifies still more their despondency and vexation by volunteering an apology for the unsatisfactory behavior of their god in taunting language, which may be thus paraphrased: "Baal does not seem to hear your petitions; but, of course, this inattention cannot be attributed to the nonexistence or the impotence of Baal, 'for he is a god.'

The Prophet of Carmel

Perhaps he is engaged in conversation with some other god, and cannot at this present moment conveniently give you an audience; perhaps he has entered some celestial 'inn' and is there taking a temporary rest, or diverting himself with a convivial repast; perhaps he is in the midst of a journey, making a royal progress through the skies; or, since even gods cannot be always wide awake, it may be that he is asleep, and so profoundly, that he requires to be thoroughly aroused; 'cry with a louder voice.'" (3Kng. 18:26,27)

Stung to the quick by these sarcasms, the prophets shriek with redoubled force, and at length, finding their cries are worthless, "they gash themselves savagely with knives and lancets," until the red blood, spouting copiously from their numerous wounds, crimsons their whole bodies with its streams. (3Kng. 18:28)

Every effort is fruitless. The sky looks down upon them as impassively as before, and not the faintest flush of any unusual glow tinges even the edges of a solitary cloud, so as to kindle in the minds of the prophets, however momentarily, a little gleam of hope. The usual time of the evening sacrifice being now at hand, Elias turns from the prophets, who had not ceased crying to Baal, and addresses the people: "Come ye to me." They instantly obey, and he then calls upon them to assist him in repairing an altar of the Lord, which had been probably destroyed by Jezabel's orders some time previously, and which was now lying in fragments upon the ground. The dilapidated altar was a significant emblem of the ruin that idolatry had wrought in the souls of the people; and Elias, by persuading them to join him in the restoration of the altar of the true God, had already succeeded in suggesting to their minds the idea, at least, of a return to their ancient religion. This favorable disposition would be strengthened by another circumstance. "He took twelve stones, according to the number of the tribes of the sons of Jacob, to whom the word of the Lord came, saying: Israel shall be thy name." (3Kng.18:31) This reparation by Elias and the Israelites of the broken altar which was completed by the symbolical twelve stones reminded the people of the time when their forefathers worshiped, as one undivided family, the very same God who was adored and represented by Elias. Thus the silent stones read them a lesson in truth, by recalling to them the sacredness and miraculous character of their own history. There was also another incidental advantage in the fact of the people assisting with their own hands to build up the mutilated altar, stone by stone. They could examine the ground and the construction, and thus be perfectly satisfied that Elias was not afraid of the minutest inspection of his materials. To whatever artifices their own prophets might be tempted to resort, in order to procure an apparent success, it was clear that Elias was guiltless of a fraud. They saw with their own eyes that delusion and jugglery were impossible. If fire came at all, there would be no alternative but to admit the genuineness of the miracle and the force of the testimony.

To make the ordeal, on his side, still more difficult and conclusive, Elias had made a trench "of the breadth of two furrows round about the altar:" a condition not imposed by him upon the Baal prophets; and he had ordered the people to pour four barrelsful of water, three times, "upon the burnt-offering and upon the wood," so that "the water ran round about the altar, and the trench was filled with water." (3Kng. 18:35)

The Prophet of Carmel

All is now ready, and the disappointed prophets, whose blood was still dripping from their lacerated flesh, stand around, with the king and the people, watching with eager eyes every part of the altar. Elias now offers up his supplication in these words: "O God of Abraham, and Isaac, and Israel, show this day that Thou art the Lord God and I Thy servant, and that according to Thy commandment I have done all these things. Hear me, O Lord, hear me; that this people may learn that Thou art the Lord God, and that Thou hast turned their heart again." (3Kng.18:36,37) The prophets of Baal were numerous, and had shrieked from morn till eve to their god without receiving any answer; their bullock lay still before them as undisturbed as when first they arranged the victim for sacrifice. Elias prays alone. He prays with a voice which, compared to the loud shouts of the Baalites, must have sounded feeble indeed. He prays once only, and behold, the heavens, as at an expected signal, suddenly open, and the lightning, rushing forth with more than usual velocity in a flaming stream, and descending earthwards falls upon the altar of Elias — a blinding cataract of fire!

The victim, the wood upon which it lay, the twelve stones, the dust, all vanish, and the very water in the trench, instead of arresting the flames, catches the conflagration. For an instant it becomes like a current of fire encircling the altar, and then the trench is dry; the water (to use the language of the Scripture narrative) was "licked up" by "the fire of the Lord." (3Kng. 18:38)

The effect of this sight upon the people was instanta-

Carmel

neous and overwhelming. Amazed, confounded, terrified, conscience-stricken, "they fell on their faces and they said: The Lord He is God, the Lord He is God !" (3Kng. 18:39)

The Rapture of Elias

Chapter Nine
The Torrent of Cison

. . . Apprehendite prophetas Baal, et ne unus quidem effugiat ex eis . . .
duxit eos Elias ad torrentem Cison, et inter fecit eos.

". . . Take the prophets of Baal, and let not one of them escape. And
. . . Elias brought them down to the torrent Cison and killed them
there." — 3 Kings 18: 40

This outburst of faith was sincere, although made under
the sudden excitement of an awful scene. But panics, even
of a spiritual kind, are soon forgotten; old habits are
strong, and the people were by nature fickle. If they were
allowed to leave Carmel in company with the Baal
prophets, who could tell how easily Elias and the miraculous fire would fade away from their memories? Who
could tell how soon the mere sight of their idolatrous leaders would bring back the diabolical fascination of that
seductive worship which they had, under the pressure of
a startling crisis, just renounced? It was not enough to fall
upon their faces through terror; wondering awe and conviction must bear immediate fruit and rise into decisive
action; confusion and shame must pass at once into the
reaction of a stern reparation. The honor of the only true
and living God had been publicly outraged by the living
ministers of false gods, and openly it must be avenged.
The forgotten law of Moses against blasphemy and idolaters must reassert its life. So long as the wicked prophets
of Baal remained to poison the minds of the people by
their teaching and example, the peril of a relapse was not
so much a risk as a certainty. But if their leaders and
seducers were completely removed from their sight and
from all possibility of intercourse, there would be a far
more hopeful probability of their remaining faithful to

their conversion. Elias, therefore, weighing all these considerations, and acting, moreover, under a higher influence than any human motive, namely, the inspiration of Him to whom life and death equally belong, gave the following command: "Take the prophets of Baal and let not one escape" (3Kng. 18:40) All had accepted the proposed ordeal with unanimous audacity, and their guilt was indivisible. To have allowed even one to escape would have compromised a principle, obscured the meaning of a judgment which was intended to be overwhelmingly impressive, and set the precedent of an iniquitous and dangerous toleration.

What a change of situation! What a reversal of the past! A few moments before and these prophets, exulting in their pride, were the objects of popular admiration and superstitious obedience. Both king and people were under the spell of their sway. Now, at a signal from that solitary, mysterious man, whom they had so often despised, they are hunted down by thousands of relentless pursuers, who refrain from slaying them on the spot, only in order that the prophet of the Lord may consecrate their death warrant by being the first to carry it out with his own hands. "When they had taken them, Elias brought them down to the torrent Cison, and killed them." (3Kng. 18:40)

This unsparing judicial slaughter is not without its lesson. True zeal is always thorough in its action. It goes straight to the point, and does not rest until it has finished its work; whereas the fervor which is mixed with human passion, or springs from an imperfect motive, is never to be depended upon. It is too lax or too severe. It makes reserves and distinctions where none ought to exist. It is capricious, and more frequently unjust than just.

The Torrent of Cison

"Let not one escape." Such was the order given by Elias to the Israelites, and we must act with the same all-embracing severity towards ourselves. We must wage an unsparing war against all sinful habits; not only those which are manifest to others, but those which are secret; not only those which damage our reputation, or injure our health, or entail the loss of money, but sins which may be committed without bringing with them any visible penal consequences in the present life. "Let not one escape." If the Baal prophets could have found time and means to have concealed themselves under some disguise, or, hidden themselves in some cave, the sentence of Elias would have been evaded, but countless eyes were watching their movements, so that flight was impossible. Now, through the corrupt weakness of our own heart, we are perpetually tempted to leave certain sins alone. Either we delay the attack until "a more convenient season," which never arrives; or we begin it and then desist before half our work is done, striking a few ineffectual blows just to pacify an uneasy conscience, but leaving the sin alive in its motive and means of nutrition. We are so unobservant of the state of our souls and of the law of God as to be quite blind to the real iniquity of our conduct; so that even grave faults thus escape notice, as foes pass in the dark unaware of the fact. We must watch, therefore, vigilantly, lest the enemies of our soul survive to torment and ruin us, when we might by a little more attention have put them under our feet. Vices, moreover, often disguise themselves under the form of virtues; thus pride apes humility, detraction pretends to spring from the love of truth and candor, revenge calls itself justice, and a criminal cowardice hides under the cloak of meekness or prudence. Let no vice escape under the guise of a virtue.

The Prophet of Carmel

It is a perilous state of mind when we have not quite determined to overcome all our known faults. For not only are we acting upon an insufficient and false principle, if we are willing to serve God in some points yet not in all, but we are exposing ourselves to a terrible slavery. If Satan can, in his wily craft, persuade men to keep just one sin actively alive in their hearts, he is comparatively content with his chances against their salvation, even if they have broken off other evil habits. If, for instance, a person gives up his former dishonesty, but continues his sensuality; or forsakes his old mendaciousness, yet allows envy of his neighbor to influence his words and actions, making him unjust and uncharitable; in these and kindred cases the great adversary of man is not by any means discouraged because the one sin which he has induced his victim to retain, while giving up others, is his fulcrum, his hook, his wedge. It is a pledge, like a marriage ring, of the still uninterrupted union that exists between the sinner's soul and the prince of darkness.

If, therefore, we desire to be free, and to dissolve such a horrible bond, we must not let a single habit of evil escape our attack. Saul "slew all the common people of Amalec," but because he spared one man, Agag their king, he forfeited his own crown. (1Kng. 15:8)

This conduct of Elias also teaches us that we must never shrink from doing our duty to God through any merely human tenderness to individuals.

Natural affection and a sympathetic clemency often seriously interfere with the glory of God. Elias personally had no harsh, vindictive feelings against the prophets of Baal; nor was he, who had shown a mother's heart in the widow's home at Sarephta, likely to find a savage satisfaction in making a river's bed gory with the blood of hundreds of executed prisoners. But he knew that his duty was to slay them, and he did not flinch. All other considerations weighed as nothing in the balance against one, fidelity to his Master.

Life was dear to those men, dearer than to the prophet, for this world could do little for his happiness; but it must be, without remorse, wrenched out of their bodies. Elias cared not who they were, noble or ignoble, old or young. Many of them may have been distinguished for talent and refinement, and, as the direct effect of their religion was to promote unbridled pleasure and luxury, they would, according to the world's standard, be genial and attractive. The prophets of the groves in particular probably had courtly manners, since they were daily guests at a queen's table. The eye of Elias, however, saw beneath their polish and sensuous elegance nothing but poisonous corruption, lying hypocrisy and blasphemous enmity against the true religion and the true God. Their office and accomplishments, whatever they were, only increased their power for evil.

Circumstances and modes of carrying out the glory of God may and do alter; but the spirit of true zeal is ever the same in its essence. There are occasions when it is our strict duty to follow, though in another form, the example of Elias. Evil in the abstract has comparatively little effect, and it is difficult to combat. It is when lodged in living men, vitalized by their minds and carried about, exhibited and communicated by their example that it acquires such a tremendous power. Satan would be much weaker than he is if he had no human apostolate. He fights truth, purity and God through the agency of our own brethren and our own flesh and blood. How often is it that we are forced to seem hardhearted to those with whom we have no wish to be at issue, and whom we shrink from needlessly offending, simply because they themselves leave us no other alternative! If, as it frequently happens, the persons whom we are thus compelled to treat as enemies should be highly useful to our temporal interest, or bound to us by ties of blood, or valuable contributors to our social happiness, the temptation to evade this painful duty is great. A false charity whispers, "Do not condemn the individual, but the vice; separate the two entirely. The world will charge you with intolerance and pharisaism. You are not called upon to judge your neighbor. Why sacrifice your interests for a prudish scrupulosity?" In cases like these nothing but a holy zeal can sustain us. We do not want to parley, or listen to the special pleading of interested motives and personal considerations. We want a current of inward force which will bear us fearlessly upon its tide, engulfing, as it rolls along, all distracting, irrelevant and contrary influences. Faith can enable us to see our obligation, but without the spirit of zeal we shall be irresolute in our intentions and feeble in our execution. We shall find ourselves at the critical moment hanging back, and with our sword of duty only half drawn from its scabbard. It is astonishing to what an extent evil is shielded from just and necessary attack, how much it loses of its gross deformity and offensive odor, if it happens to be enshrined in the personality of those with whom we are connected by the various links of life. Affection for and dependence upon others are apt to blind and unnerve us in the great battle for righteousness which we are called upon to fight before God and man. We allow earthly love and mere self-interest to erect their idols in our hearts. We are too tender in dealing with these seductive foes; and though we profess to be on the side of God, we too easily dispense with the stern duty of destroying evil without mercy wherever we come across its path. Elias triumphantly raised his altar upon Carmel, and the people confessed their faith in the true God; but the victory would have been incomplete if he and the people had not brought the wicked prophets "to the torrent of Cison, and slain them there."

The conduct of Elias in putting the idolatrous Baalites to the sword has been condemned by certain sceptical critics as an act of unnecessary cruelty, as a barbarism utterly indefensible on any enlightened principles. To this observation no further reply is necessary than that the prophet acted under the inspiration of that God who had in the case of drought made the elements obey his prayer, and had just before put an additional seal to his divine authority by the miraculous descent of fire upon Carmel. But this calumny upon the character of Elias suggests a reflection. They who are zealous for the cause of God must be prepared for unjust accusations; they will be attacked by enemies, and often misunderstood by friends. They will be called under certain circumstances hard and cruel, when in reality their apparent severity is but the rough side of a justly indignant love, the love of God. Holy zeal is often mistaken for pride, when it is one of the fruits of humility. They who have it appear, on the surface, to be arbitrary and exacting, whereas none are less so, for they have dethroned and crushed self in order to make room in their hearts for the cause which they have embraced and represent, and which through them demands its rights. When zealous men are accused of egoism and of making themselves too prominent, what is the true explanation? They are full of energy and fire, and as they move along, their individual form is brought distinctly into view; for no matter how much they try to keep in the shade, they cannot escape the illumination reflected upon them by the pure light of their good works. Zeal is called obstinacy by those whose crime is that they are themselves wanting in firmness or principle, and a righteous wrath is stigmatized by the tepid as an intemperate outburst of human passion when, if there be excitement, it is but the natural quivering of the moral arrow as it speeds rapidly to its mark, under the sacred impulse of duty.

Chapter Ten
Watching for Rain

. . . ecce nubecula, parva quasi vestigium hominis, ascendebatde mari.
". . . behold a little cloud rose out of the sea like a man's foot."

— 3 Kings 18:44

The proceedings of that memorable day on Mount Carmel, lasting as they did from morning till evening, must have heavily taxed the strength and also the feelings of Elias. The slaughter of the prophets must have been a wearisome and sickening work, and most men would have been glad to take some repose and food. But Elias cared little for his own wants. His first thought was not about himself, but about the awe-stricken king. "Go up," he said to Achab, "eat and drink, for there is a sound of abundance of rain." (3Kng. 18:41) He wished Achab to take an immediate repast, for he knew that he must be exhausted by the waiting, the fasting, the exciting suspense to which he had been subjected for so many hours, and finally, by the startling scene of the fire descending from heaven, during which the king must have trembled for his own life when he saw the awful flames skirting so closely the spot on which he stood, all being followed by the bloody execution of the prophets.

The king at once obeyed Elias. "Achab went up to eat and drink." (3Kng. 18:42) Let us consider these words, which Elias uttered before leaving Achab's side: "There is a sound of abundance of rain." How supernaturally sensitive was the prophet's ear! "There is," not shall be, "a sound of rain." Yet at that point of time there was nothing to indicate to any ordinary observer the welcome fact. The loud

whir of the coming downpour had not commenced; no gur-
gling came from the channels of the mountain streams to
show that they were again filling; not a raindrop had moistened a leaf in the woods; not even a vapor light as a silvery
shadow could be traced in the whole expanse of the heavens. Still the prophet spoke truly when he said, "There is a
sound of abundance of rain."

Can we not read a parable as well as an historical truth
in this acute listening of Elias? Faith and love have a marvelous power to quicken the intelligence of the soul. The
just can hear the sound of the active presence of God in
many of the events of the world, when they who think
little about God perceive nothing but the ordinary
mechanical course of nature or the obscure eccentricities
of chance. The spiritual ear recognizes easily a divine
melody in doctrines which represent only confusion and
discord to men whose unassisted reason is their sole and
self-chosen organ of understanding. Many who are completely immersed in the distracting noise of this life are not
likely to learn anything except what the world can tell
them in its own misleading language. "If thou wilt incline
thine ear, thou shalt receive instruction; and if thou love
to hear, thou shalt be wise." (Eccu. 6:34) But how can they
incline their ear and love to hear true wisdom who are
deaf to all but appeals to their unmortified nature?

"There is a sound of abundance of rain." Sometimes
when we think of the difficulties which we have to
encounter in our pilgrimage here, we are apt to be dis-
heartened, but let us listen well to the teaching of faith. We
cannot, it is true, with our natural powers, hear the happy
songs of the just, and the voice of the Lamb speaking to
His beloved ones, and bidding them "follow Him whithersoever He goeth"; yet to faith how distinct and certain is

Watching for Rain

the echo! How it rings sweetly and encouragingly down into the battlefield of this valley of tears! How it supports the hands that droop, and the feeble knees that bend totteringly under the burden of duty!

As soon as Elias had declared to Achab that he heard "the sound of abundance of rain," he did not follow the king's example by going up "to eat and drink;" his next step was to pray. "He went up to the top of Carmel, and casting himself down upon the earth, put his face between his knees, and he said to his servant: "Go up and look towards the sea." And he went up and looked, and said, "There is nothing;" and again he said to him, "Return seven times." Then in an instant "a little cloud[1] rose out of the sea, like a man's foot," and as soon as it caught the watcher's eye and was reported to Elias, he knew that it was the herald of a rapid outburst of waters. (3Kng. 18:42-44) Again his first thought is about the king: "Go up and say to Achab: "Prepare thy chariot, and go down, lest the rain prevent thee." Scarcely had Achab had time to listen to the message from Elias, when a sudden change in the sky warns him to hasten his departure. "Behold the heavens grew dark with clouds and wind, and there fell a great rain." (3Kng. 18:45) Mounting, therefore, hurriedly, his chariot, he is quickly

[1]According to the fathers and commentators the little cloud seen by Elias from the summit of Carmel, rising from the sea bringing rain and fecundity, symbolized Mary. Beneath the veil of this miraculous cloud the inspired gaze of the prophet foresaw the mysteries and the greatness of the august Virgin. The S.C. of Rites (May 31, 1919) approved the Proper Prefaces of Our Lady of Mt. Carmel and St. Elias for the Carmelite Order. In the first we read: "Deus; Qui per nubem levem de mari ascendentem, immaculatam Virginem Mariam beato Eliae Prophetae mirabiliter praesignasti, etc.," thus adding the approval of Holy Church to this interpretation. (Editor's note.)

The Prophet of Carmel

on his way to the city of Jezrahel. Where now is Elias? Look not for him at the side of the king; look not for him in the rude but often welcome hiding place of one of those caves or retired dells with which Carmel proverbially abounded.[2] He has left the spot where he has just been praying with so mighty an effect, and is traveling in the same direction as Achab — traveling also, like him, rapidly. But no chariot, either of king or king's courtier, bears his limbs, weary with his long and recent fatigues. He is on foot, "The hand of the Lord was upon him, and he girded up his loins, and ran before Achab till he came to Jezrahel." (3Kng. 18:46)

How strong and yet confusingly perplexed must have been the king's emotion at a sight so strange! The great prophet, miracle-worker and sword-bearer of the living God on foot, and he himself riding! Fain would Achab have taken him up, but he has no opportunity, even if Elias were willing, for quickly as the lashed and alarmed horses gallop through the increasing rain and wind, the white foam

[2] "Though they be hid in the top of Carmel, I (the Lord) will search and take them away from thence." (Amos, ix, 3) Tradition still points out the Spelunca Sancti Eliae, a spot held in great veneration by Christians and Mohammedans alike, and which the Carmelite fathers have transformed into a chapel where Mass is said. Rivaling this grotto in interest is the cave called the "School of the Prophets." Its rocky walls are covered with inscriptions in Hebrew, Greek, Arabic and Turkish. The Greek inscriptions are the most remarkable from the standpoint of paleography; the angular form of the letters proves that they date from the first centuries. The Bollandist, Fr. Carpentier, acknowledged that since their discovery, Papebrock's thesis can no longer be maintained. The learned Orientalist, Dr. Scholz, published these inscriptions for the first time in 1821. They prove irrefutably the existence of Christian hermits on Mt. Carmel in the earliest years of our era, and strikingly confirm all the Carmelite traditions. (Editor's note.)

which flies from them marking, as with snowflakes, the dim track of their course, still more quickly speeds the prophet. Now his gaunt form is for a moment seen cleaving the gloom; now it melts away like a spectre and is lost; to and fro it sways under the eddying whirls of the wind, until it seems as if the prophet must sink, overwhelmed, to the ground. Bravely, however, he battles on, for he is upheld by a fortifying desire. Achab will soon be exposed again to the seductive influence of Jezabel. He will be liable to forget, in the presence of other persons, objects and occupations, the solemn events of Carmel; so Elias wants to engrave the thought of himself, in connection with Carmel, deeply upon the mind of the king before he enters that Jezrahel where his idolatrous queen is awaiting his arrival. He has also another purpose; he wishes to show that, though he has brought down, by his prayers, fire and rain from above, yet he is but a servant of his God, and in that service is equally ready either to be the lackey of a king who only a few hours ago was a rebellious apostate from the true religion, or to open the heavens by his word. At length the walls of Jezrahel are reached, now assuredly there is shelter at hand; now the famous royal ivory palace (3Kng. 22:39) will not be too good to serve as a resting place for Elias. The chariot stops, Achab looks round and descends. Where is the prophet? He has vanished. In vain there is a call for lights and a diligent search: that wicked city was no home for him, it was enough to have come as near as its gates; so, after finishing his humble task as Achab's courier, he has turned rapidly back and gone again — unrested, unfed, unhoused — into the thick darkness, the blinding rain, and the furious wind.

Chapter Eleven
Fear and Flight

. . . Sufficit mihi. Domine, tolle animam meam, neque enim melior sum quam patres mei.

". . . It is enough for me. Lord, take away my soul; for I am no better than my fathers." — 3 Kings 19: 4

Thus far nothing but moral greatness has characterized the conduct of Elias. Every deed has been that of a saintly hero. He has run his course like a giant. Even giants, however, can stumble, and there are spots upon the sun. It is a fact as startling in its antecedent improbability as it is full of warning to us all, that after his signal victory over the idolatrous prophets, Elias lost suddenly his former courage. It broke under him like a frail reed. He who had not known a tremor in the deep solitude of the brook Carith; he who alone, in the face of hostile thousands, had stood up on Mount Carmel, and dared them to the test of fire from heaven; he who had raced the king's chariot in the whirl of a raging tempest up to the very gates of Jezrahel, actually reeled at the tidings brought to him by a messenger from a woman. In what singular contrast does the bearing of Jezabel stand with that of the prophet! As soon as she hears of the slaughter of her favorite prophets, her iniquitous heart, instead of being cast down with dismay, is fired with indignation and revenge. Struck as she was, she at once darts in return the arrow of a deadly threat against the slayer. Blood shall have blood without delay. "Such and such things may the gods do to me, and add still more, if by this hour tomorrow I make not thy life as the life of one of them." (3Kng. 19:2) The words were but the expression of a passionate resolve. They only

The Prophet of Carmel

came second-hand through the lips of another, who probably trembled himself as he delivered them to his listener; and yet, as they fell upon that listener's ear, his boldness seemed to dissolve as under the influence of a spell. "Then Elias was afraid."[2] The mere shadow of the pagan queen's wrath was actually heavy enough to paralyze the prophet of the living God; nor was it a mere passing vibration of the nerves. "Rising up, he went whithersoever he had a mind."[3] Panic was his master. He fled forward without a plan or distinct idea of any kind, like a leaf driven along by the caprice of the wind, until he found himself far in the desert. There he stopped, bewildered, exhausted and utterly despondent. Jezabel and her sword were behind him and a barren wilderness before him. His late victory seemed now a failure, and the future looked worse than the past; so, crouching under the shade of a juniper tree, his only longing was to breathe out his wearied soul into the hands of his God. It was some consolation that he had escaped from the plotting hands of Jezabel's executioners, and that his death, under such circumstances, had not been a public triumph for the cause of idolatry. But now that he had saved his life, it seemed to him scarcely worth the keeping. Each hour of existence only reminded him of his misery. Like a wounded deer just straggling onwards in its lonely agony, until it has found some secluded, leafy nook in which to lie down and expire, he felt that the spot which he had chosen was no unsuitable resting place for his last moments. Barren appeared his efforts to sustain the cause of the true God, and so it was well to die in a desert, whilst the thorny juniper tree would wrap him round solemnly and gently

[2] Ibid. 3, 3.
[3] Ibid.

with its peaceful though scanty shade. "It is enough for me, O Lord," he moaned forth, "take away my soul, for I am not better than my fathers." (3Kng. 19:4)

If we have learned much from the prophet's former zeal, we can also learn much from his present weakness. The sudden failure of Elias in courage is a striking warning against overconfidence in the actual state of our soul, however favorable it may appear. When Elias was upon Mount Carmel how little did he dream of the change that was so rapidly to come over his mind! The precise cause of his cowardice we do not know. Had something earthly been mixed up with his zeal for God at the beginning, or drained into it, through self-reflection, afterwards? Had he slightly forgotten that, if he had been so preternaturally bold, he owed all his force to God? Had God purposely withdrawn His grace in order that the prophet might feel more deeply than ever the utter dependence of man upon God, and his own intrinsic weakness? We do not know, but certain it is that the prophet was allowed to be humbled by fear and despondency.

Who can tell what the morrow will bring forth! No past victories over temptation, no advances in holiness, however great, can guarantee us against a future fall. Often we fancy ourselves proof against a strong assault, and we suddenly collapse under the weight of a feather. One day we break through iron bars, and on the morrow we are imprisoned in the filmy network of a spider's web. Goliath thought that if ever he were to be overcome, it would be by an onrush of numerous and well equipped foes; he fell beneath a pebble cast from the sling of a beardless youth. Peter cut off the ear of Malchus in the presence of a band of armed men, and yet denied his Master through fear of a young maidservant's bantering tongue.

The Prophet of Carmel

There are two dangers which we must earnestly avoid: an over-sanguine reliance upon our past successes, and forgetfulness that, unless we incessantly pray for fresh strength, our old force will evaporate, and we shall find ourselves in critical moments weak, and "unstable as water."

The conduct of Elias warns us also of the difficulty in preserving tranquility and courage when our course is not perfectly clear. When God revealed to Elias his duty, and gave him definite commands and a distinct work, he walked securely. Fear came upon him precisely when the future was uncertain. There was a short pause in the divine communications, and the prophet was left to himself. His duty was to wait patiently for more light, but just at this time of comparative stillness, and when he had no manifest task to accomplish, the message from Jezabel arrived. None knew better than Elias the powerlessness of the queen to hurt a hair of his head against the will of God. Yet, as sounds in the hush of night seem louder than they actually are, and as objects looming in the dim twilight impress the senses with an idea of vastness of which half is illusion, so the mind of Elias, unillumined as it was at the moment by any definite command from God, magnified unduly Jezabel's threat. It is not nearly so hard to be courageous when our path of duty is perfectly clear before us, and our eye is steadily fixed upon a plain mark, as it is to be courageous when we have to wait for light, and perhaps suffer until the will of God be unmistakably known. To be benighted in a forest is a more arduous position than to have to toil up a steep and rugged mountain in broad daylight. In the latter case, the goal is ever before us, and we are preoccupied with our exertions; in the former, our imagination, left to itself and working incessantly, creates dangers on every side, with no limit except our fancy or our nervousness. Elias had two difficulties to contend with; his path was for a while not perfectly clear; he had to wait in the dark, and, besides that, he had to endure the persecution of Jezabel. When we have a definite task to fulfill, and when we know thoroughly what that task is, its nature and its exact difficulties, we brace up our souls accordingly. We multiply our prayers, and we ask the prayers of others. We have recourse to distinct means in order to carry out our well-defined end. We keep a close guard and direct our energies towards one point, until the storm has passed over. So far all goes on well; we struggle and conquer. But how will it be with us if these circumstances alter? How will it be if the definite present is exchanged for an obscure future? How will it be if, instead of the stimulating excitement of action, we have to remain immovably quiet or to prepare for possible yet uncertain contingencies? It is well known that, after a successful battle, a victorious army may sink into weakness, merely because the combatants are obliged to remain for a time inactive. Give them at once another opportunity for fighting, give them an enemy whom they can see, measure and grapple with, and their spirits will continue buoyant; whereas to be still, to watch for the slow development of events, is often demoralizing. It is the beginning of disaster. Hence it is that a retreat, however necessary as a military exigency, and however skillfully conducted, is notoriously perilous, and, when safely accomplished, ranks higher than many victories. Men who are heroes in the midst of the fiery rash of clashing squadrons become weak, wavering and craven under the ordeal of a retrograde movement.

When the army of the first Napoleon withdrew from the burning ruins of Moscow, it was not so much the long, sharp lances of the Cossacks that carried devastation into

The Prophet of Carmel

the ranks of the French as the wearisome march through never-ending, monotonous snow, the hoarse howling of the wolves that kept hovering around the stragglers, and the blank uncertainty of what was in store for the survivors. Terrible as the actual reality was, its dark colors grew darker still as they passed through the morbid imagination of men whose bodies were enfeebled by hunger and toil, until the bravest wept like children, and staggered mechanically along, each man recognizing, with a mingled curiosity and alarm, in the spectral forms and countenances of his fellow fugitives, the portrait of his own altered self.

However painful may be the trials of our courage which God permits us to undergo, they will be of incalculable use if we draw from them the right lesson. Like a winnowing fan, they separate the chaff of our motives from the wheat. What we frequently mistake for genuine courage is nothing but an accident, or a lucky coincidence of events, or a confidence which, swelling pretentiously out of some merely earthly cause, subsides under the slightest pressure.

As long as we are in our ordinary groove of life, we are apt to miscalculate our strength. Routine and circumstances are our buttresses; and when they change the props fall, and we find ourselves on the ground, to our confusion and dismay.

Many a Christian goes on well in his religious duties, and even sets a bright example, so long as his surroundings are akin to his tastes. Let these be changed, and his light vanishes or turns sickly and dull. It came more from without than within; it was a reflection rather than an independent and interior lamp. For instance, this man prays well, and is radiant with confidence as long as he is in good health; give him sleepless nights, weary days, deprive him of his

Fear and Flight

usual recreations, separate him from friends, and then see if his fervor and assurance are not woefully diminished. The state of his blood-corpuscles had more to do with his former condition of mind than spirituality. Another person delights in an active life; to be still is torture and imprisonment. He is here, there and everywhere; he organizes charities — organization, he tells you, is his *forte*; he interests friends and strangers in various good works, of which he is the center. Unquestionably he does a great deal of good; though, perhaps, his energy might be less fussy and audible. Let this model specimen of philanthropic energy be placed in a totally different situation; let him be put under a shade, where his particular kind of light must burn unseen if it burn at all; let his pet schemes be criticized and opposed; or let them fail because, even when others are more capable of fulfilling the office, he insists upon having the whole management in his own hands, as if the glory of God would not be complete without the ornamentation of his monogram; let the physical excitement, the conspicuousness and exterior importance of his actions, and the applauding sympathy of onlookers, be taken away; then what a collapse there will be of that man's moral strength, whose zeal could only run in a self-chosen, uncovered channel, and who cares not to dig another!

There is but one security against a disheartening breakdown in the hour of trial, but one remedy for cowardice, but one fountain of vigor that will not dry up under the change of events. Our motive in all things must be the will of God. "I have meat to eat which ye know not of," said Jesus Christ to His disciples, "My meat is to do the will of Him that sent Me, that I may perfect His work." (Jn. 4:33) As God changes not in the midst of His perpetually changing creation, so they who do His will partake of the divine inflexibility in the midst of the ever varying phases of life. Every other motive except that drawn from the desire to serve God will only deceive us at first, and ruin us at last; it will be like an artificial rock made of paper or cork, whereas he who keeps the commandments of God walks with God Himself, and is borne up by the "everlasting arm." If we want to test our strength, our courage and our endurance now, before our trials come, we have simply to ask whether we are, by the grace of the Holy Ghost, and in union with Christ, trying to do "all things to the glory of God."

Let us not rely upon our natural character, our assurance, or our circumstances. Above all things, let us be humble in our estimation of ourselves. "He that thinketh himself to stand, let him take heed lest he fall." (1Cor. 10:12) We may imagine that we are safe, because in a favorable combination of events we have as yet shown no signs of failure. But can we wait when to wait is a severe cross to our impetuous temper or passion for activity? Can we bear to sow much and reap little? Can we endure to be lonely, hidden "in a hole of the rock," when we crave for a warm hand and an encouraging voice? Can we support the sight of evil triumphant and goodness oppressed? Can we bear the spoliation of our property without harboring revenge against the robber? Can we bear patiently to have our fair fame shattered at a blow by some audaciously precise calumny, or slowly nibbled away by constant subtle innuendoes, which we scarcely know how to grasp and strangle? Believing ourselves to be of considerable importance to a particular person or cause, can we submit charitably and resignedly to be passed by unnoticed, perhaps to be rudely trodden upon by the very feet which we often kissed? If, in these and similar cases, we are apt to think too highly of ourselves before we have been tried, let us remember Elias. How brave he was, denouncing a king, and slaying hundreds of his prophets; how mighty, raising the dead, and shutting and opening the heavens as though he had the keys of the skies; yet it is this same man whom at another time we see flying, panic stricken, from a woman's threat, and hear mournfully wailing forth these despondent words: "It is enough for me. Lord, take away my life."

"It is enough for me." This is not the language of faith, not the language of hope, not the language of perfect obedience. "It is enough for me" sounds strange in the mouth of one who was the special servant of God. If it was enough for Elias, was it also enough for his Lord? That question should have been answered first. Elias in this respect has many followers. "It is enough for me," so thought the patriarch Jacob when he heard of the supposed death of his child Joseph. All his children were gathered together to comfort their father in his sorrow. Nevertheless, he would not be consoled, but said, "I will go down to my son in hell (the grave) mourning;" and yet he lived to behold Joseph as the chief ruler in Egypt. (Gen. 37:33-35; 46:30) So thought Job when he exclaimed: "Why is light given to him that is in misery, and life to them that are in bitterness of soul, that look for death, and it cometh not?" Yet "the Lord gave Job twice as much as he had before, and the Lord blessed the latter end of Job more than the beginning." (Job 3:20, 21, 42:12) "It is enough for me," so thought the great Apostle when he prayed thrice that the thorn in the flesh might be removed; and yet to him came an answer from heaven: "My grace is sufficient for thee; for power is made perfect in weakness." (2Cor. 12:9)

The Prophet of Carmel

How often is the cry of Elias repeated by those who are
weary of the world, worn out by their labors, battered by
temptation, sick of themselves and of others; and yet how
constantly does God in His wisdom and mercy turn a deaf
ear to their supplication! He who, in His love, puts upon
His children the cross, can alone tell when it is best for
them to be released from the yoke. If our divine Lord had
come down from His cross when His murderers invited
Him to descend, where would have been our salvation and
the exceeding height of His glory? Elias despondently asked
for death, and was answered by a miracle which reinforced
the springs of life. The complaining of the servant, with its
half unconscious undertone of reproach to his Master for
having allowed him to be so severely treated, was met with
more than gentleness instead of sharp rebuke. Twice Elias
fell asleep under the juniper tree, hoping probably that
each time the slumber would insensibly deepen into the
stillness of the grave, and the shadow of the tree pass into
that of the valley of death; and twice was he awakened by
the tread of an angel, and sustained by heaven-made food.
"Behold, there was at his head a hearthcake and a vessel of
water; and he arose and ate and drank, and he walked in
the strength of that food forty days and forty nights unto
the Mount of God, Horeb." (3Kng.19:8) Had Elias been
taken at his word, and died in his weariness as he wished,
how imperfect would have been his appointed work, how
discordant the close of his career with its beginning, and
how shorn of much of its extraordinary splendor would
have been his sanctity! His own choice, if granted, would
have left him lying on the sands of the desert, the friend-
less corpse of a broken-hearted man, to be the prey of
some passing wild beast, or the rude sport of Jezabel's
minions if they came that way upon his track. How little

did he imagine that instead of such an end, God was preparing for him the chariot of fire, and a mysterious dwelling place into which, as yet, the breath of mortality has not entered! Let no one exclaim too soon, "It is enough for me," and before God Himself has given the *Nunc dimittis* to His servant. We may gain our prayer, but we know not what higher things we shall lose. In the midst of the driest desert there is ever at our side an angel, though unseen, waiting to touch each of us, and to say, "Arise and eat, for thou hast a long way to go." Elias was allowed to remain for a little while under the juniper tree, but he was not permitted either to expire under its shadow or to make it a loitering place of unnecessary rest. The Mount of Horeb, the ancient site of the burning bush and the revelation of the Law; Horeb, the special place of the manifestation of God, was his next destination, and, therefore, he was told to "arise and eat," in order that he might reach it without fainting on the way. The sleep, the food and the juniper tree were only transitory means to that end.

The tree in the desert is an apt symbol of life; it is not our Horeb, for our true Horeb is heaven; but it lies in the pathway to it, and in a wilderness, the wilderness of our present state as exiled children of Eve, through which we must go up to that mount of God where will be our future exaltation and eternal rest.

It may be only a poet's fancy that the shade of the juniper is injurious to man, but its roots are certainly bitter, and the tree can, of itself, give little if any nutrition. So also no chemistry can extract any immortal food out of this world alone; if we rely upon it entirely we perish. Neither must we give to it our chief love, for even if we keep our eyes fixed upon the distant Horeb we shall never

The Prophet of Carmel

reach the sacred peak unless we "arise and eat and walk" steadily towards it "days and nights," that is, throughout our whole life, from its dawn until its setting sun. But though the present world cannot furnish us with divine strength out of its own elements, and although its best refreshment passes away like a shadow, yet here, and here alone, is the necessary support to be found. The hearthcake and the water were only found by Elias near the juniper tree and in the desert, but they were placed in that spot by the angel of God at His command, and they were placed at the prophet's head as thus symbolizing that the soul's nourishment, although miraculous, is nevertheless provided for man upon this visible earth. Moreover, that which is spiritual is given to him under material forms, just as the power which carried the exhausted Elias forty days and forty nights to the Mount of Horeb was mysteriously drawn from the "hearthcake and the vessel of water." Though the prophet took food twice, there was only one cake of baked bread and one vessel of water—a figure of the unity of grace amidst its manifold sufficiency for the various wants of the soul, and preeminently of the unity of that "One Bread" which is the transcendental gift of the new kingdom of Christ. "O Christian, remember thy dignity" (St. Gregory) and thy true destination. Mistake not the desert for the mount of God; life is short, and thou hast a long way to go; life is thorny, and apt to poison thee with its vapors if thou slumberest too profoundly beneath the scanty covering that it offers; evil lurks amongst its branches and the tempter finds there a covert for his ambuscades, and a spot from which he can easily make his seductive appeals. But fear not; "Why art thou sad, O my soul?" (Ps. 41:6) One greater than any angel is near to help thee with His pierced hands. He will quench thy thirst with the word of His truth, the consolations of the Comforter and the tenderness of His pardon. "If any man thirst, let him come to Me and drink." (Jn. 7:37) He will feed thee with His own Flesh, that Flesh which, having once passed through the disfiguring furnace of His bitter cross, is now without intermission ever passing through the furnace of His eucharistic love, and ever being laid upon an earthly altar by the ministrations of a mortal priest, Its ravishing glory being annihilated as long as It remains hidden beneath the disguise of what appears to the senses only a common, hearthcake's form.

Chapter Twelve
The Vision at Horeb

. . . Zelo zelatus sum pro Domino Deo exercituum . . .

". . . With zeal have I been zealous for the Lord God of hosts . . ."
— 3 Kings 19:10

Arrived at Mount Horeb, the prophet took up his abode in a cave. As he was one day pondering over the strange events of his life, and wondering what the future would bring forth, the hush of his usual solitude was suddenly broken by a supernatural voice, asking a question that must have electrified him into immediate and anxious attention. Had he been a man whose mind at that moment was wandering dreamily in the mystic regions of fancy, he must have fallen straight from the clouds, like an eagle pierced by some strong arrow shot from an unseen archer's bow. "The word of the Lord came unto him, and He said to him, What dost thou here, Elias?" (3Kng. 19:9) There are questions that, in a few words, speak volumes, questions that turn the eyes of the soul, with a concentrated vision, straight upon itself; questions that, by their deeply suggestive and unerring appositeness summon a man instantaneously before the tribunal of conscience, and pour a stream of light upon his present position, his duty, his thoughts and his feelings. Such was the inquiry, put to the prophet. It lifted him up, as the angel seized Habacuc by the hair of his head. (Dan. 14:35) and carried him swiftly over all the thoughts, fears, hopes, motives and actions that had resulted in his flight to Horeb. It showed him by a single phrase the bearing of the past upon the present, and bade him look well into the separate

115

threads of the link uniting them together. "What dost thou here? Art thou come hither from Carmel by My express command, or hast thou drifted hither scarcely knowing how or why? What dost thou here? Is the lone cave thy proper sphere of duty? Is it only a fresh hiding place, or is it a new starting point? A refuge, or another novitiate? Art thou come here to carry on, still more energetically, war against idolatry and idolaters? Or art thou sorrowing unprofitably over bygone woes?" Every syllable of the question had its significance, and since the prophet was not only alone but was addressed by name, there was no possibility of evading or parrying it. "What dost thou here, Elias?" The force of any question is increased when the speaker calls the person spoken to by his name. Familiar as our own name is to each of us, it is one of the very few words which, however worn by constant use, never loses its vitality. It is a chord of sympathy which always vibrates to the slightest touch. Our name may be to others a mere sound, suggestive of nothing distinctive, easily and quickly forgotten, but to the individual, his own name is a potent reality. Counsel acquires more weight, rebuke bites with more keenness, and kind expressions pour forth more sweetness, if they are invested with this personal appeal. Whenever our name is uttered, it perpetually renews within us the sense of our existence as rational beings, and often deepens the feeling of our responsibility in whatever state of life we may be. If only whispered gently, it will sometimes recall the wandering brain to its lost center, and awaken the dying sleeper when other more elaborate means have failed. Our name is part of our own self. It is the epitome of our varying life, the audible consciousness of our identity. Adam must have felt an additional thrill when, as he and his guilty partner were hiding themselves "amidst the trees of Paradise," the "afternoon air," awful in its very softness, wafted to him the sound of his own name. "The Lord God called Adam, and said to him, Where art thou?" (Gen. 1:8,9) So it must have been with the child Samuel in the Temple, when "the Lord called Samuel." (1Kng. 3:4) So with Lazarus in the tomb, when the voice of Christ pierced its stillness with, "Lazarus, come forth." (Jn. 11:43) So with the traitor Judas, when in the torch-lit gloom of Gethsemane he heard the unanswerable question: "Judas, dost thou betray the Son of Man with a kiss?" (Lk. 22:48) So with the Magdalene, when from the lips of the "gardener" came a well-known voice, saying, "Mary!" in a tone which revealed at once her risen Lord. (Jn. 20:16) So with Peter, whose soul must have been rent with unspeakable emotion and poignant memories when the final commission, "Feed My sheep, feed My lambs," was prefaced with "Simon, son of Jonas, lovest thou Me more than these?" (Jn. 21:15-17)

The question that was put to Elias may be usefully repeated in these days by others to themselves. It was tipped, arrow-like, with the pointed sheathing of his own name, in order to give it a special directness and force. If in the pagan times of Greece and Rome the child's name-day was a religious festival, if the Jews were accustomed to connect it with such a solemn act as the initiatory rite of admission into the Mosaic covenant (Lk. 1:59), what should be the aspect under which we regard our Christian name — we, the children of a kingdom compared with which paganism was thick darkness, and Judaism only preparatory twilight?

If any one has a name full of meaning, a name which ought to affect him in a way different from other words, a name which should rouse him from spiritual sloth, and

The Prophet of Carmel

remind him of his true end and dignity, it is assuredly that which he received at the font. The Christian name was pronounced at the mighty moment when the regenerating water flowed over him, and its sound mingled with that august language by which is expressed the triune nature of God. "I baptize thee in the name of the Father, and of the Son, and of the Holy Ghost!" What tremendous proximity! What an association of the creature with the Creator, of the redeemed sinner with the Redeemer, of the name of man with that of God!

Let not this Christian name ever be sullied by actions unworthy of its history. Let it never be quoted as an example sanctioning rebellion against that King to whose service it has been eternally devoted. Let it never be profaned by lips whose unlawful familiarity is a sign, not of pure affection, but of corruption and of fellowship in sin. Let it be unknown in places of dangerous resort, but be a household word in the mouths and habitations of the good. Imagine that Jesus Christ calls each of us by name, and says: "What dost thou? Art thou doing anything for Me, or only talking, and promising, and dreaming? Art thou, alas, doing something or many things against Me?" O man, born for eternity! Art thou living as if this world were thy real home instead of being only a place of pilgrimage, a battlefield, a race, a valley of penance? O vain, luxurious, indolent man! Is this sin smitten earth, which the Man of Sorrows has stained with His Blood, a fitting place for conceited dreamers and sensual loungers? It is meant for penitents, who, knowing that heaven is only to be taken by violence, "work out their salvation with fear and trembling," (Phil.2:11,12) before "the night cometh, when no man can work." (Jn. 9:4) But "what dost thou here?" O Catholic, who, through no merit of thine, knowest the "one faith," and art in the "one body of Christ," and hast abundant means of grace; thou from whom much will be required, because much has been given; (Lk. 12:48) "what dost thou here" with all thy gifts and opportunities?

Now is the time for putting these probing questions, whilst we are still alive. In a little while the time for questions will be over, and the only voice that we shall hear will be that of a final sentence: either, "Come, ye blessed of My Father, possess you the kingdom prepared for you from the foundation of the world," or else, "Depart from Me, you cursed, into everlasting fire, which was prepared for the devil and his angels." (Mt. 25:34-41)

Elias, in reply to the question, "What dost thou here?" made no allusion whatever to his fear of Jezabel as being in any respect connected with his present condition. This dread had probably lost much of its intensity. His journey, the miraculous food, and his solitude had all contributed towards allaying his panic. Boldly, yet calmly, he lays before God the plea, which he desires to be at once an explanation and a defense of his conduct. His zeal was his ground of justification, and it was also his stumbling block, for the more he hated the ungrateful iniquity of the Israelites, the more bitterly did he feel the apparent failure of all his efforts on the side of righteousness. Like the Psalmist, he "pined away" at the sight. "I beheld the transgressors, and pined away because they kept not Thy word." (Ps. 118:58) This is his answer: "With zeal have I been zealous for the Lord God of Hosts, for the children of Israel have forsaken Thy covenant; they have thrown down Thy altars; they have slain Thy prophets with the sword; and I alone am left, and they seek my life to take it away." (3Kng. 19:10)

The Prophet of Carmel

Scarcely had he thus contrasted the overwhelming triumph of wickedness visible to his eyes on one side with his own sensation of weakness, abandonment and helpless isolation on the other, when a vision came before him which must have wrapped his whole being in awe, and in which he unexpectedly read a sublimely striking commentary upon his own words. As he stood on that desolate rock, "before the Lord," a mighty wind passed near him, a wind so strong that it seemed as if it would have carried away with one resistless gust the whole mountain and the very heavens themselves. (3Kng. 19:11,12) The heights shook, staggered and left their massive foundations upturned and bare like an oak wrenched up by its roots. The hard rocks crashed fiercely together, and were shivered like frail glass into pieces. Then came an earthquake, and as the quivering ground parted asunder, the eyes of the prophet looked giddily down into abysmal depths, which gaped wide, and closed again, like some living monster into whose jaws the trees and rocks were sucked. "After the earthquake came a fire," rushing with terrific velocity from every quarter at once, flashing from sky to earth, and earth to sky, "running along the ground," (Ex. 9:23) "devouring the cedars," (Judg. 9:15) and "enveloping all things far and near as with one vast shroud of flame, until the mountain burned into heaven " (Deut. 4:11) and the air was the blast of a furnace which seemed to have no bounds. When the "great and strong wind," had ceased "over-throwing the mountains and breaking the rocks in pieces;" when the reeling and yawning earth had poised itself, closed up its fissures, and again become firm; when the scathing heat, lurid flames, and sulphurous smoke of the fire had vanished; there came the soft whisper of "a gentle air." It was a change strikingly marked in its nature, impressive in its effects upon the spectator's mind, and full of mystical significance. The wind, earthquake and fire seem to symbolize more particularly the awfulness of the omnipotence and majesty of God; whilst the "gentle air" represents the mercy of God, the delicate breathing of His tenderness and compassion, the caressing touch of His ineffable Fatherhood. The former remind us of the "terrors of the Lord," which the thunder, lightning, clouds, smoke and trumpet blast produced upon the people of Israel when upon that very same mountain the Law was proclaimed. The latter is typical of Bethlehem, with its heavenly calm, and of that noiseless moving of the Holy Spirit over the souls of men, to which these words in the Canticle may be applied: "Come, O south wind, blow through my garden, and let the aromatical spices thereof flow." (Cant. 4:16)

As the wind, earthquake and fire shadow forth the Old Dispensation in contrast with, and as a preparation for, the Gospel, so it may be said that they are figurative in a more general sense of the often rigorous discipline through which God is obliged to work upon the stubborn and sluggish hearts of men to fit them for the gracious gift of His more intimate presence. Hence it is said that God was absent from the more tremendous of the elemental forces. The Lord God was "not" in the wind, "not" in the earthquake, "not" in the fire. These were only the mighty heralds of God, the advance guard of the Lord of Hosts, the levelers and pioneers of the highway of the great King, the signals of His coming. When God Himself arrived, He indicated His presence by a figure which conveys to the mind nothing but peace, gentleness and comforting assurance. The wind, earthquake and fire produced a terrifying impression upon the senses. A confusing and appalling sound came from them. It was only "the gentle air" that was followed by an articulate, intelligible and, as it were, human voice. This shows that God wishes Himself to be known especially as a Father, and as such to speak with His children. He rejoices when He can dispense with the painful yet necessary discipline of fear. He is Love, "God is Love," and He delights to reveal Himself in that character to us. He passes us in the tempest, earthquake and fire; He dwells with and in us through love. Elias had gazed with uncovered countenance upon the tremendous agitation of the heavens and the earth. He was a spectator in whom a brave curiosity was largely mingled with awe. He felt, too, that there was a bond of kinship, a moral likeness between these elemental forces and his own disposition; they were strong weapons and modes of decisive action which harmonized with his inner self. But as soon as he heard the "gentle air," he was no longer an onlooker; he knew that this was the presence of the Lord God, so "he covered his face with his mantle." This hiding of his countenance was more than usually significant. It was a confession of his utter nothingness in the presence of God. It was a dutiful and deliberate shrinking of the creature from the tremendous closeness of the Creator. It was a sign of his intense desire that nothing earthly, however fair or sublime, should at such a moment intrude itself upon his attention. If his eyes were as unworthy as they were unable to see God, they should at least be debarred from beholding anything else when He was so near. The covering up of his lips, eyes and ears in the deep folds of his rough garment was a kind of figurative death and burial of the outer man, showing that when the soul wishes to listen to God, it withdraws itself as far as possible from every avenue through which the sounds, the scenes and the influences of the world can enter. It abandons, in spirit, the tabernacle of the flesh and, wrapping itself around with the pall of mortification and recollection, its higher life quickened by this death, it is prepared, like the prophet, to hold undisturbed communication with God.

Elias and Eliseus

Chapter Thirteen
Breaking of the Clouds

. . . Derelictus sum ego solus,
et quaerunt animam meam ut auferant eam.

". . . I alone am left: and they seek my life to take it away."

— 3Kings 19:14

The first words which Elias heard, as coming forth, he stood at the entrance of the cave, were probably not what he had anticipated. Instead of something new, the same question which he had answered before was again put to him: "What dost thou here, Elias?" The repetition of the question gave him an opportunity of reconsidering his former reply, and was an act of condescension on the part of God. If his previous words were spoken in haste, if they were the too-uncontrolled moaning of disappointment at the seeming failure of his endeavors to stem the wickedness of Israel, here was an opportunity for him to make a more deliberate explanation. If he desired, he might now cancel, or at least modify, his original language.

A vision had passed before him in which he was reminded of the omnipotence of God in a way most appalling even to himself. If God did not destroy Jezabel and all the idolaters of Israel by some signal display of retributive justice, it was clear that He refrained, not through want of force, but of will. The tempest, the earthquake and the fire, which must have made the prophet feel as if the very world was being broken up, were but as toys in the hand of the Almighty. If, therefore, He allowed His own honor to be blasphemed, and His own prophet to be persecuted, there could be only one solution to the mystery: this abstention was part of the infinitely wise, yet incomprehensible, scheme of the divine government. God must have had ends in view, and means for those ends, which He had chosen to hide from His servant.

Considerations such as these would have been forced upon the mind of Elias by the scenes that had passed before him. Had the tremendous drama taught him nothing? Had the "great and strong wind" cleared away no mists from his brain? Had the earthquake shaken none of his erroneous impressions? Had the fire thrown no light upon events, and burnt up none of his unsubstantial fears? Had the "gentle air" soothed in no degree his indignation or his grief? It would appear not, for Elias after the vision does not vary his answer by one syllable. The topic is still the same, the complaint the same. His heart is still broken at the thought of the wickedness of the Israelites, and his own helpless isolation. He is so consumed with zeal that he tosses about like a man in a strong fever. Looking round he beholds no sign of interference on the part of Him for whose sake he is burning with this fever; nothing heavenly comes to his aid, and nothing earthly. "With zeal have I been zealous for the Lord of Hosts, because the children of Israel have forsaken Thy covenant; they have destroyed Thy altars, they have slain Thy prophets with the sword, and I alone am left, and they seek my life to take it." (3Kng. 19:14) Such is still his language.

In spite of the prophet's serious fault in speaking again with such a tone of despondency, it is impossible not to recognize the sublime qualities that lie beneath it. He knows that he loves God, and he is not afraid to appeal to that love as a justification of his complaint. He suffers because the law of God is dear to him and its violation tears his heart. His very loneliness is caused by the utter destruction, as he supposes, of the other faithful prophets

Breaking of the Clouds

of God. There is no concealment of his thoughts, no diplomatic glossing over of his case, no reserve. He lays the state of his soul frankly open to his Master, and leaves Him to deal with it as He judges right. Nor is Elias mistaken in his confidence. God forgives much to those who love much. Not a word of direct rebuke is addressed to the prophet; his fault is passed over in silence, as if God were unwilling to add another drop of bitterness to his already full cup of woe. Instead of reproving him sharply for his complaints, or dismissing him from His special service, God reassures and encourages him with the most tender condescension. He sends him at once on a fresh mission, and unfolding to him some of His future plans for avenging His outraged law, enjoins him to "anoint" a prophet who shall be his successor, and also two kings[1] whose swords are to smite powerfully the enemies of the true religion. He reveals to him that, instead of being alone, there are numbers of Israelites alive who are still untainted with the pollutions of Baal. "I will leave Me seven thousand men in Israel who have not been bowed before Baal." (3Kng. 19:15-18) As long as Elias was left to his own broodings and fears, his estimate of realities was both fallacious and depressing. His mind sickened in the atmosphere of his own imaginations, and the future seemed darker even than the present. God speaks, and all is changed. His vitality returns, the weight upon his spirit grows lighter and the clouds roll off. Before, all was perplexity, and he thought of nothing but murdered prophets and ruined altars; now, the dawn of a more hopeful change begins to flush the horizon with its golden rays.

[1] Hazael, king of Syria, and Jehu, king of Juda. The prediction and command were not fulfilled actually by Elias in person, but by the agency of Eliseus. (4Kng. 8:13, and 9:1-6)

The Prophet of Carmel

"I alone am left, and they seek my life to take it." This had been his final conviction, the summing up of his many sorrows, and in a moment, rising out of the darkness and the void, two kings, and a second Elias, and seven thousand fellow witnesses to the living God, stand in clear outline before his mental vision.

It is a mistake to suppose that God is necessarily forgetting, or abandoning His servants, because we, in our blindness, cannot, at the moment, see any escape from the difficulties which surround the accomplishment of His will. One of the natural tendencies of zeal is to imagine that the cause of God is closely bound up with our own persons and our own endeavors. The more intensely we fix our minds upon gaining a certain pious object, the more firmly we are convinced that it can only be attained in that particular manner which commends itself to our present judgment. Elias no doubt thought that as his own efforts in favor of the kingdom of God seemed to be fruitless, there was nothing more to be done. He was the only pillar left, and that one pillar was on the point of being cast to the ground by the unchecked force of his enemies. "They seek my life to take it." Yet the greatest saint amongst us is but one out of numberless instruments that God chooses to employ.

We are but poor bits of clay, that the divine Potter lays upon the wheel of His providence, to be used or cast aside as He sees fit: the wheel going on the same, with or without us. With zeal we must ever join a strong spirit of indifference and of faith. Of indifference, so that if God, for wise purposes of His own, chooses not to employ us in that particular way which we imagine to be highly important to His interests, we may not be disappointed, but, on the contrary, rather glory in His rejection of our services. Of

Breaking of the Clouds

faith, because otherwise we shall be the dispirited slaves of sight, and sink under the phantom load of difficulties which God can, if He pleases, scatter with a breath. Zeal, without great confidence in God's wisdom and power, becomes often a torment rather than a force, and is the cause of endless shocks, disappointments and failures.

We should have a deep respect for the zeal of good men, notwithstanding the errors with which it is frequently accompanied. It is so rare, especially in a skeptical age like the present, to find anything like a holy passion for the cause of God, that when we do meet with an individual in whom the fire of devotedness burns with vehement ardor, we ought to welcome him with special honor, and assist his aims with cordial cooperation. Men who are full of love for the glory of God, like enthusiasts of other kinds, often fall into errors of judgment through their eagerness to gain their point. They do not, for instance, always perceive accurately whither they are going; they are, perhaps, rough and clumsy in manner, deficient in tact and too impatient in their treatment of others, who, not possessing their own generous spirit, stand provokingly in their way. They have not always the time, even if they have the disposition, to be careful about the niceties and proprieties so much admired by those to whom life is rather a pleasant drama than a tremendous reality. Carried along by some highly important and absorbing idea, they think little of trampling upon inferior interests, if they be in the way of their own onward march. Whatever the defects of zealous good men, we ought to learn to make every possible allowance for them on account of the excellence of their motives. God treated the shortcomings of Elias with exceeding leniency, and few things are more repugnant to the spirit of charity than the

The Prophet of Carmel

detestable habit of criticizing and depreciating the conduct of fervent men, merely because that fervor is not always as perfect in practice as it is pure in intention. Open and avowed antagonists who fight you face to face and inch by inch, are far less offensive and injurious than those passionless critics who, whilst agreeing with you in principle, are ever on the watch, microscope in hand, to point out the minutest flaws, real or imaginary, in your course of action. There are persons who have little or no respect for even undoubted heroism, unless the hero himself belongs to the approved caste, and wears the regulation uniform. Zealous men naturally expect to meet with opposition, both intense and malignantly willful, from the powers of hell, and from the "manifest children of the devil," (1Jn. 3:10) but their most hampering and depressing obstacles come from the dead weight of the lukewarm, the carnal prudence of the timid, the caviling of the habitual fault finders, the tyrannical etiquette of the formalists and the gloomy foreboding and prophecies of the pessimists. These are stings which have, before now, made many a saintly "lion of the Lord" writhe with pain and slacken his pace, although they have failed to drive him from the path marked out for him by duty and love.

Chapter Fourteen
The Prophet's Mantle

Elias. . . reperit Eliseum, filium Saphat . . . cumque venisset Elias ad eum misit pallium suum super illum.

"And Elias . . . found Eliseus the son of Saphat . . . And when Elias came up to him, he cast his mantle upon him." — 3 Kings 19:19

From the cave on Mount Horeb, and the vision which passed before the prophet, the scene now changes to a quiet spot where the plough is silently turning up the soil. Who would have imagined, as the patient oxen move along, that when they come to one particular part of the field, a great event would suddenly take place? Often had Eliseus, the son of Saphat, been there before, when driving his plough, and nothing unusual had ever occurred. Perhaps he was at that moment wondering how the next crop would succeed, whilst his eyes were carefully watching the course of the plough, when he feels something fall upon his shoulders. What can it be? Some one has flung an old mantle upon him. An old mantle! How poor and insignificant a thing it seems! Yet that mantle is a power; it commands with authority.

It is a visible prophecy and a sublime consecration. It will revolutionize that man's whole life. It will transport him from his oxen and his furrows to another sphere, almost to another world. The ploughman shall henceforth become the prophet's servant, companion, friend and mighty successor. He shall no longer wait anxiously upon the seasons, and look into the bowels of the dull earth. A higher destiny is opening to him, and the time will come when he shall foretell the future, command the very elements and quicken the dead by the mere touch of his lifeless bones.

The Prophet of Carmel

How wonderful are the ways of God! How unexpected and mysterious are His appointments! How His hand darts unawares into the circle of a man's ordinary occupations and, drawing him forth, lifts him up to the undreamed height of a stupendous career! Such was the case with Eliseus: "When Elias came up to him, he cast his mantle upon him." No words were said, but the son of Saphat knew the deep meaning of the act. "He forthwith left the oxen and ran after Elias." The oxen were his property; ploughing was his immediate occupation; and his parents were alive, but he forsook all. Nor did he go slowly as one sad at heart. "He ran after Elias." He only asked one little favor: "Let me, I pray thee, kiss my father and my mother, and then I will follow thee." (3Kng. 19:19,20) Sublime as was the office to which he was called, his filial heart turned magnetically for an instant to the thought of his home. He wished to soften the abrupt separation by a few affectionate words; and so, though quite willing to go at once with Elias, he begged for just one farewell kiss for his father and his mother.

Elias, knowing that this desire was the genuine fruit of pure natural affection, and not an excuse for weakness or selfishness, willingly yielded to his request. At the same time he added a note of caution, for he knew well the disturbing effect of human love even in generous, self-sacrificing hearts. The final kiss might possibly unnerve his will by setting in movement a current of feeling against which it would be hard even for grace to struggle; so when Eliseus left his side, he fortified him by a strict command: "Go, and return back, for that which was my part I have done to thee." (3Kng. 19:20) If in the New Dispensation our divine Lord seemed to be on one occasion more severe than Elias was in the Old, it was because He saw in the would-be disciple a disposition which rendered it unsafe for him even to go and bury his dead. Eliseus was of another stamp. Not only did he return, but out of that stern separation from his home he made a festival of joy and boldly effaced the associations of the past. He not merely left his cattle, he did more — he made others to be witnesses of his abnegation and sharers of his delight. "He took a yoke of oxen and killed them, and boiled the flesh with the plough of the oxen, and gave to the people, and they did eat; and rising up he went away, and followed Elias, and ministered to him." (3Kng. 19:20)

As we contemplate the conduct of Eliseus, it is impossible not to feel a painful contrast between the cheerful generosity of his spirit and our own too-frequent repugnance to follow a Prophet and Master far greater than Elias. When Jesus Christ seeks us out, and casts on us that sacred mantle of some higher vocation, do we not frequently show a strange reluctance to recognize His will? Sometimes we falsely pretend that we are not sure whether it is His mantle that has touched us or only our own imagination. Sometimes we throw it off impatiently as an unendurable yoke, although it has been long worn by our Lord Himself, and bears on it the blood marks of His Passion. Sometimes we turn round to Him for a moment, just long enough to confess our responsibility, and then, looking Him full in the face, but with one hand still fixed upon the plough of our ordinary employment, we go on without further attention to His call. Unlike Eliseus, we are full of excuses and eloquent in pleading for a dispensation. God never invites any man to a higher life, never asks any one to take up a cross and deny himself, without first strengthening his soul with grace sufficient for the appointed work. But we look so exclusively

The Prophet of Carmel

at our own imperfections and our merely natural capacities, that we disbelieve the heavenly message and its accompanying gift of supernatural strength. So Jonas reasoned when, instead of going to Ninive as soon as he had received the divine command, he fled "from the face of the Lord, and went down to Joppe." (Jon. 1:3) We know the result — he was flung headlong into the sea out of the very ship into which he had for safety embarked. So reasoned the man in the parable who hid his talent in a napkin; he was condemned for his sloth as "an unprofitable servant," and "cast into the exterior darkness." (Mt. 25:26-30)

Eliseus did not argue that, because he was only a ploughman, he was, therefore, utterly unequal to be the minister of the mighty Thesbite. He forthwith left "the oxen and ran after Elias." Too many Christians, on the contrary, refuse to change their past habits even for Christ's sake. They cling to the narrow field of their old occupations and pleasures; or they try to make a bargain with Christ, offering to follow Him on one impossible condition, namely, if they are allowed to carry their yoke of oxen with them wherever they go! What is the end of all this meanness and cowardice? Some part from Christ entirely, and are at last fastened forever to the plough of Satan, in that awful field which bears no harvest but continual woe. Others, even if eventually saved, suffer nevertheless an irreparable loss of grace, of merit and of glory far beyond any measure within the reach of their calculation. God desires them to be more perfect, to aim higher and do more than they have hitherto accomplished for His glory, but He will not exalt them against their free will; so they spend their lives in the cramped furrows of commonplace views and material satisfactions. They toil

The Prophet's Mantle

on in the world more like the dull earth on which they tread and fix their downward gaze than like sons of God and heirs of heaven. They follow oxen when they might have "taken wings as eagles." (Isa. 11:31)

Chapter Fifteen
The Coveted Vineyard

. . . Da mihi vineam tuam . . . et ille ait:
Non dabo tibi vineam meam.

". . . Give me thy vineyard . . . And he said: I will not give thee my
vineyard." — 3 Kings 21:6

The course of events connected with the life of Elias
brings us now to another dark spot in the career of Achab.
In the city of Jezrahel there lived a faithful Israelite called
Naboth. He had a vineyard, of whose extent or value nothing is recorded. But of one thing we are certain: however
insignificant it may have been, Naboth prized it as an old
inheritance. It had come down to him from his forefathers.
He had probably played there in his early years, and
watched with a child's eagerness and joy the gathering of
the ruddy grapes. The vineyard was a link in the chain of
his own life, and when he came by succession to be its actual owner, he felt in all its intensity the sacredness of the
trust. The Mosaic law was to him a divine command and,
according to its precepts, such an inheritance could never
be sold except under the pressure of a most extreme necessity. In any case, if parted with, it must return, in the year
of Jubilee to the line of possessors. (Lev. 25:10,28) This
vineyard was in a situation that would, in ordinary circumstances, have been thought to be fortunate rather than otherwise. It was in a select quarter, for it was close to Achab's
palace, and constantly under the royal eye. Strangers in
passing would naturally ask whose property it was, so that
Naboth's name would be favorably known as the king's
neighbor. As often happens, this very prominence became
a serious misfortune. King Achab, by frequently looking at

The Prophet of Carmel

Naboth's vineyard, conceived a strong desire to convert it into a garden of herbs and make it part of his own grounds. He was just fresh from his two victories over the Syrians and had not the slightest idea of being opposed by one of his subjects in any matter, especially in such a petty question as the annexation of a corner of land. He thought the transaction would be both an honor and an advantage financially to Naboth, for he offered him either a "better vineyard" or "the worth of it in money." To his astonishment and indignation, Naboth declined the proposal. (3Kng. 21:1-3)

With him it was not a question of sordid profit and loss, of more vessels of wine in his cellar, or more money in his coffers. It was a question of principle, of religion and of loyalty to his ancestral blood and rights. To part with his vineyard, even to a king, would be treason to his God. If such a necessity were forced upon him, he would regard it as a calamity to be deplored and prayed against: "The Lord be merciful to me, and not let me give thee the inheritance of my fathers." The firmness of Naboth disconcerted the king, so he left him without saying a word in reply. But the image of the longed-for possession haunted his mind. His splendid gardens, his "ivory house," and his triumphs in battle gave him no satisfaction. There was a flaw in them all that prevented his soul from settling itself in peace. Naboth's vineyard was wanting, and the desire for it rose under Naboth's opposition into a strong temptation which mocked him fiercely; so that on his return home, "casting himself upon his bed, he turned away his face to the wall, and would eat no bread." What a picture is this of the slavery of sin! What a warning against uncontrolled indulgence in any unlawful wish! At first the thought came into Achab's mind, probably on some day

The Coveted Vineyard

when he was quietly walking in his palace grounds, that it would be rather convenient if he could make an arrangement for the acquisition of Naboth's vineyard. He did not wish to be overlooked and his privacy disturbed. The symmetry of his garden would be improved and there would be a greater supply of herbs, pleasant in their savory fragrance and succulent for the royal kitchen. This thought, by being brooded upon, assumed larger proportions and more definite shape. It began to glow with life and color. From a faint suggestion it passed into a fixed wish, and from a wish it became a passion. This conqueror, who had lately seen his army destroy a hundred thousand of his enemies in one day, and had heard their king promise to restore all the cities that had been taken from his father, was actually carried away captive by an inanimate piece of earth. It sapped the life from his heart. He refused food and, as sick persons often do before expiring, he shunned the light of day and turned his melancholy face to the wall. Who is there that has not known something of this process? Who is there that has not learned by bitter experience how easily an object most trifling in itself can break up the soul's former peace? It appears nothing at first, and it is nothing; yet, if the desire of it be allowed to remain unchecked, it displaces far greater things than itself. It roots itself in the very depths of the mind; it tints all the world with its own color, and the soul, sad and fainting with hunger, turns to the wall, as if life were not life as long as the coveted object is out of reach.

If we are tempted by an unlawful desire, it is of great importance not only to keep its mental form out of the imagination as well as we can, but also to avoid whatever is likely to suggest it to the mind. To say to ourselves that we dislike the dangerous thought and yet to be perpetually

The Prophet of Carmel

hovering or lounging about its neighborhood is mere self-delusion. Achab's palace was in seductive proximity to the coveted vineyard. "Give me thy vineyard," he said, "because it is nigh and adjoining my house."

Achab's proposal is an illustration of one of the favorite arts of the tempter of the human race. Achab did not profess any intention of depriving Naboth of his property; that would have been too tyrannical. He offered to make an exchange, and an exchange in favor of Naboth's material interests. "I will give thee for it a better vineyard; or if thou think it more convenient for thee, I will give thee the worth of it in money."

When Satan wants to persuade a man to commit some sin, he begins by directing his mind to a false point of view. He adjusts the moral telescope for him, and giving it the proper diabolical inclination and aim, he brings the glass to bear, not upon God and God's law, but upon self and earthly considerations. "I will give thee," says the tempter to his victim, "a better vineyard; or if thou think it more convenient for thee, the worth of it in money." Here is the first step towards perdition, allowing the soul to look away from the will of God, and to make its choice by the narrow standard of what seems most suitable to the wants of the "old man;" a standard which suits admirably the devil's interests, under the mask of its being a real advantage to man, just as Achab politely talked of Naboth's convenience when he meant his own. The bait which is dangled before the prey is the improvement of his position. The poor man is promised a release from indigence if he will only steal or cheat. The ambitious man is to mount higher on the ladder of life if he will only violate the rights of charity or justice, and put his foot upon the ruins of both. The slothful man is to enjoy his ease if he will only neglect that labor which is the necessary condition of duty. In these and similar cases, the supposed advantages are magnified, and not a word is breathed about the terrible loss which follows upon the exchange. Naboth would have had his superior vineyard if he had consented to Achab's request, but at what a price! At the cost of his conscience, his honor, his religion and the friendship of that God whose laws he would have broken! Thus Esau, when he was faint after the toil of the chase, no doubt relished the "red pottage" of Jacob, but he lost the first birthright and his father's blessing; the savor of the broth made him, for the moment, forget the real nature of the transaction. So it is with all sin. The devil, like a skillful juggler, distracts the attention while he accomplishes his end. With one hand he ostentatiously makes man a present of some worthless trifle, and with the other he robs him of that soul which was bought by the Precious Blood of Christ.

The danger to Naboth arose from the fact that his property was close to that of the king. This proximity would not have been an evil if the king's character had been different. A good monarch would have admired Naboth's fidelity to his God. Naboth's peril, therefore, was due to two causes combined, the nearness of his vineyard to Achab's palace, and Achab's envious and rapacious disposition. He was not content with what he possessed, but was ever on the watch to increase his domain by absorbing into it that which belonged to others.

Herein is a further illustration of Satan's character and his relation to ourselves. Since the fall of the first man, he has tempted, corrupted and ruined a countless number of souls, yet he is and must be ever insatiable. Men live and die, and generation after generation succeeds, but Satan remains unchanged in his hatred and unwearied in his

The Prophet of Carmel

pursuit of victims. He is not distant from us, though unseen. He is the prince of this world, and we all dwell within the range of his keen eye. He can talk to us without making any audible sound, and make advances to us without the necessity of human witnesses. No documents of transfer are needed; the soul can pass into his hands, and none but ourselves be aware of the transaction. Men often think that they have not sold their soul, but only dallied with his offers, or lent it for a time, when the bargain has, in fact, been signed and sealed, and will never be revoked, because the hour of penitence will never arrive. If we depend upon ourselves; if we are thoughtless, and do not know the sacred value of our vineyard; if we treat our souls and bodies, our goods, our time and our natural powers as if they were absolutely our own, and not a trust from God; if we care to what use they are applied, so long as we can obtain a momentary gratification in exchange for that misuse, then we are certain to fall. The vineyard which has been planted by God Himself, and tenderly watched and watered, will be uprooted, and in its place there will be a desecrated spot, in which Satan, the new and tyrannical master, will walk and gather his own bitter herbs at will. As the prince of this world endeavors to seduce individuals, so also he is ceaseless in his efforts to seduce, if it were possible, the Catholic Church herself. He tries to persuade her to barter away the inheritance of the faith for toleration of errors. He promises the protection of the civil power on condition of the sacrifice of divine authority. As Naboth knew well the exact position, measurement and boundaries of his own vineyard, where it began and where it ended, so the Church of God is the infallible judge of the nature and limits of her own rights, as well as their faithful guardian. Satan, on the other

The Coveted Vineyard

hand, tries to confuse the boundaries between what is human and what is divine. He audaciously claims for the world that which is unmistakably God's, and where bribes prove unavailing, he resorts to persecution by force. Age after age the struggle goes on; individuals yield; and Satan is the victor, but the Church herself never wavers. "Give me thy vineyard," says Satan, now blandly, now fiercely, and the unchangeable answer is always returned: "I will not give thee my vineyard."

Had Achab been left to himself, it is possible that he might have interfered no further with Naboth. But on this, as on other occasions, a prompter was speedily at his side, whose superior boldness, cunning and malice exercised an overwhelming influence upon his mind.

Chapter Sixteen
The Iniquitous Plot

Dixit ergo ad eum Jezabel, uxor ejus: . . . Ego dabo tibi vineam Naboth Jezrahelitae.

"Then Jezabel his wife said to him: . . . I will give thee the vineyard of Naboth the Jezrahelite." — 3 Kings 21:7

As the king, with his face turned to the wall, was writhing under his disappointment, and with contemptible childishness giving way to grief, he suddenly revived at the whisper of a woman's voice. It was the queen who, gliding like an evil spirit to his couch at the critical moment, came to pour a deadly cordial into his heart. "Then Jezabel his wife said to him: Thou art of great authority indeed, and governest well the kingdom of Israel. Arise — and be of good cheer! I will give thee the vineyard of Naboth the Jezrahelite." (3Kng. 21:7) Mark the mingled flattery and arrogant assumption of Jezabel: "Thou art of great authority, and governest well," yet it is to her usurpation of his authority that he will be indebted for gaining his iniquitous desire: "I will give thee the vineyard." Achab, so far as we know, made no inquiry as to the means by which she intended to accomplish this object. His instinct told him that they could not be innocent. Jezabel, he knew, had no delicate scruples about right and wrong. If, in order to effect her purpose, it were necessary to tread through blood, she would plunge her feet boldly into the red stream, and walk straight to her mark without a shudder or a blush. Like many sinners, who are quite willing to take advantage of the superior nerve and malicious ingenuity of others, and yet wish to escape being openly compromised

145

The Prophet of Carmel

themselves Achab thought it most discreet, and perhaps most dignified, for there is an etiquette even at the devil's court, to make no remarks upon Jezabel's offer. He did not say "No," for he would then have lost Naboth's vineyard. He did not say "Yes," for he would then have become avowedly a partaker of her crime. He did not ask any questions, for questions in suspicious matters have an awkward quality. They bring up information with their hook, but they also bring up at the same time responsibility and guilt. Achab, therefore, shut his eyes, and said nothing. Probably he tried to persuade himself that his own hands would remain clean if he adroitly turned his back, though Jezabel's scheme was marked by an atrocious combination of hypocrisy and cruelty. "She wrote letters in Achab's name and sealed them with his ring, and sent them to the ancients and the chief men that were in the city, and that dwelt with Naboth." (3Kng. 21:8) The purport of these letters was to order the chief councilors to condemn Naboth on the false charge of blasphemy against God and the king. There was something preeminently diabolical both in the idea and the details of this crime. Naboth had braved the king's anger because he was faithful to the law of Moses, so he is charged with blasphemy against the God of Israel, that God whose holy rights he was upholding. By firmly refusing Achab's bribe, he prevented, as far as it depended upon himself, a royal violation of the divine law, so he is denounced as a traitor to his king. To give extraordinary weight to this double accusation, the mockery of a solemn fast is proclaimed, and the victim is placed conspicuously amongst the chief of the people. Opposite to him, with perjury stamped upon their shameless brows, sit "two men, sons of Belial," who bear "witness against him before the people." (3Kng.21:10-13)

The Iniquitous Plot

The double character of the charge, its base falsehood, the subornation of the witnesses, the perversion of judicial authority, the appeal to the people and the profession of religious zeal which masked the impious motive, remind us vividly of much later times, when the scene was laid in the judgment hall at Jerusalem instead of Jezrahel, and when a greater than Naboth was arraigned and condemned. Wicked as the whole plot was, its hideous blackness was deepened by another element. It was a heathen woman, the devotee and high patroness of the sensual idolatry of Astaroth, who, under the forged name and seal of her husband, the king of Israel, pretended to avenge by a religious murder the fiction of a crime alleged to have been committed against the true God. Jezabel's plan succeeded. The pliant judges and "the sons of the devil" did their work well. Naboth's innocence, fidelity and courage were no shield against iniquity armed with force. Never again was Naboth to return to his home; never again was he to hear, at the joyful vintage time, the merry shouts and songs of the gatherers as they plucked the grapes, or "the voice of the treaders" (Isa. 16:10) as they crushed the rich fruit in the press. The heritage of his fathers would behold him no more. He had done what he could to prevent it from passing into the hand of strangers, but all in vain. Like many other servants of God, he must protest and die. "They brought him forth without the city, and stoned him to death," as if guilty of blasphemy. (Lev. 24:16)

Nor was Naboth himself the sole victim. In order to effectually prevent the possibility of the vineyard being claimed by his heirs, they also were silenced by death on the same day, probably at the same hour. The blood of the children may have mingled, as it flowed, with that of the

The Prophet of Carmel

father — one common stream soddening the same earth,
telling to it the same ghastly tale, and crying out for retri-
bution with one united voice. (4Kng. 9:26)

As soon as Jezabel heard the tidings, she went straight
to Achab. Here again we may note the rapid, business-
like energy of her character. She lost no time in excuses
or explanations, she gave no encouragement to dreamy
musings upon the past. Sentiment was out of place now,
even if Achab were inclined to indulge in it, as he seemed
to have been when "he turned his face to the wall," and
fretted. Let Naboth's corpse look after itself; Achab's
business was to seize the dead man's vineyard. She said
to Achab, "Arise, and take possession of the vineyard of
Naboth the Jezrahelite, who would not agree with thee,
and give it thee for money; for Naboth is not alive, but
dead." (3Kng. 21:15) There is a dash of effrontery and
apologetic suggestiveness in these words which brings
home to us most graphically the reality of this history.
What could be more characteristic than the allusion to
Naboth as the man who, like an inconvenient fool, would
neither "agree with the king" nor sell his property for
money? She speaks of the murdered victim with the
utmost indifference, and reminds the king of his name
and his opposition, as if he had perhaps almost forgotten the whole circumstances of the case. Naboth was
alive, and is dead, that is all. The stones had battered
his limbs and sprinkled his brains far and wide, until
death released his just soul from the body's wreck. But
Jezabel was silent about that. The practical point,
according to her ideas, was the fact of the man's death;
and the logic, the moral of the fact for Achab was,
"Arise, and take possession."

The Grotto of Elias

Chapter Seventeen
The Unexpected Meeting

. . . Inveni eo quod venumdatus sis ut faceres malum in conspectu Domini.

". . . I have found thee because thou art sold to do evil in the sight of the Lord."— 3 Kings 21:20

Eager to secure his prize, Achab ordered his chariot to be prepared, and on the day after Naboth's death left Samaria, where he was staying, to go to Jezrahel. He was attended by two companions, and doubtless he talked with them freely and joyously about the object of his journey. No thought of the murdered man's spirit rising up and crossing his path troubled his mind: "For, because sentence is not speedily pronounced against the evil, the children of men commit evils without any fear." (Eccl. 8:11) Blind infatuation of the wicked! Could Achab have foreseen the future, he would have shrunk with horror at the idea of inviting two persons to accompany him, of whom one especially was destined to play an important part in the avenging providence of God. It was by a prophetical rather than a fortuitous coincidence that, following in another chariot closely behind Achab's, (4Kng.9:24) or in the very same chariot with him,[1] sat "Jehu, the son of Josaphat, the son of Namsi," (4Kng.9:2) and his comrade and future captain, Badacer. Little did Achab imagine that he was taking with him to Naboth's vineyard the very man whose arrow (4Kng. 9:24) should one day pierce the heart of Joram, Achab's son, who had become king of Israel, and would order Badacer to fling his corpse with dishonor into the

[1] Josephus, Ant. ix, 6, § 3.

The Prophet of Carmel

identical field where Naboth was stoned to death. Strange and terrible was the punishment of his guilt. Not only did Jehu kill Joram, but it was also by his command that Achab's wife and queen, Jezabel, was cast headlong from her window, so that "the wall was sprinkled with her blood, and the hoofs of the horses (of Jehu) trod upon her." (4Kng. 9:33) It was this same Jehu also who "slew all that were left of the house of Achab in Jezrahel, and all his chief men, and his friends, and his priests, till there were no remains left of him." (4Kng. 10:11) When men mock God by their bold disregard of His laws, He not infrequently mocks them by the awful irony of an impending judgment, of which they are, at the moment of their crime, utterly unconscious.

Aman little dreamed that the gorgeous robe in which he had expected that King Assuerus would have ordered him to be arrayed would be placed, as a consequence of his own frustrated devices, upon the hated Mardochai, and, what was most galling, placed there by his own hands. Still less did he anticipate the more terrible punishment that was awaiting him, "like a thief in the night." He forgot in his merriment that "whatsoever a man soweth, that also shall he reap." Aman was delighted with the suggestion of his wife Zares and his friends, that he should have a gibbet erected for Mardochai. "The counsel," we are told, "pleased him." Nor was it to be an ordinary vulgar beam, but one "fifty cubits high." What was the fruit of his plotting and his pleasure at the boldly ingenious idea? "Aman was hanged upon the gibbet which he had prepared for Mardochai." (Est. 7:10)

Everything went on smoothly with Achab up to a certain point. To inspect and take official possession of his new property was easy, for no person disputed his claims or

The Unexpected Meeting

interfered with his proceedings. In high spirits he now leaves the vineyard, untroubled with the reflection that its title-deed is the fruit of an atrocious crime, and hastens back to Samaria to assure Jezabel that he has faithfully carried out her advice, and to enjoy her congratulations upon their mutual success. His steeds bound rapidly along as soon as they leave the gates of Jezrahel. On every side the people, when they see the chariot approaching, make room with a profound obeisance for the King. There is a single exception. One man, either from audacity, blindness or infatuation (for until the chariot advances more closely it is hard to determine the cause), stands motionless in the very line of the royal track, more like a rock than a living being. Nearer and nearer the chariot comes, louder and louder the noise of the wheels, until, at the very moment when you would expect to see him crushed in the dust or hurled to a distance, the impetuous horses swerve, and are abruptly reined up by the driver's powerful yet trembling hand. What is the meaning of this involuntary arrest? Why does the king's countenance, lately flushed with the excitement of his evil delight, turn pale with fear? Has the murdered Naboth risen from his recent grave, and terrified both horses and charioteer? No, but the king is confronted by an apparition scarcely less startling and equally unforeseen. Before him is a form which he recognizes with appalling certainty. Do his eyes deceive him? He wishes in vain that they did.

Many years have passed since that memorable night after the tremendous scenes upon Mount Carmel, when the prophet of the Lord ran before Achab's chariot up to the very gates of that same Jezrahel which he has just left, and mysteriously vanished amidst the darkness and roar of the tempest. From that hour to this the two had never

met, but there is no mistaking that face. It had once
looked kindly upon Achab, when the long wished-for rain
poured down in answer to the prophet's prayer. Now, its
expression is changed. It disconcerts and alarms him.
Naboth's blood that has been shed has silently cried to
God for justice. The cry has been heard, and the answer
has arrived in the person of Elias. There he stands, right
in the king's path, as if he had risen up through the
ground, alone as usual, and with his countenance charged
with an unearthly sternness, akin to the message which he
had come there to deliver from God. Had Achab dared,
he would have fled past him without pausing to listen or
to speak. Had Jezabel been at his side, she would have
urged him to seize the opportunity, and slay him without
delay. But the conscience within his breast, a conscience
not entirely seared, and the commanding attitude of
Elias, left him no alternative but to stop.

The fact of Elias meeting him at such a time and occasion was an ominous circumstance. Before the prophet
had uttered a word, Achab felt that, in spite of himself, a
chill was beginning to freeze his spirit. The presence of
Elias boded no good to a guilty man, whether king or
peasant. But whilst Achab was alarmed, he was also
stung; and under the impulse of a half nervous, half
rebellious excitement, in which fear, vexation and the
instinctive writhing of a guilty soul were mingled, he first
broke silence by launching at Elias a question which had
in it the unmistakable ring of the old scornful mood.
"Achab said to Elias, Hast thou found me thy enemy?"
(3Kng. 21:20) There was a time when Achab was furious-
ly seeking for Elias, in order to slay him; and when he had
seen him, he said: "Art thou he that troublest Israel?"
(3Kng. 18:17) Since then a change had passed over

The Unexpected Meeting

Achab. He evidently now regarded Elias as the pursuer, and himself as the pursued. This showed that his conscience had not altogether lost its sensibility. It spoke loudly enough to make him aware of his criminality. Yet enough of his former disposition remained to nerve the speech addressed to Elias with a tone of boldness, partly real and partly affected, in order to disguise his actual uneasiness.

The prophet, as on a former occasion, met the question with a trenchant frankness. He shot his bolt straight at the mark. "I have found thee, because thou art sold to do evil in the sight of the Lord." (3Kng. 21:20) Sold to do evil! Few words could more concisely express the state of any great and habitual sinner. He commits iniquity in order to enjoy, as he fancies, more liberty; and losing all the true freedom which he before possessed, he becomes the worst, lowest and most miserable of slaves. "Know ye not, that to whom you yield yourselves servants of sin, his servants (i.e., slaves) you are whom you obey, whether it be of sin unto death, or of obedience unto justice?" (Rom. 6:16) Hard to bear as any kind of compulsory service is, yet there need not be in it any moral degradation. The chain and the lash cannot of themselves pollute the soul. Men maybe "sold," and their labor may, justly or not, produce material good to both individuals and states. But to sell ourselves by our own free will into a slavery, of which the only product is wickedness here and eternal death hereafter, to sell ourselves after having been purchased out of bondage by the redeeming Blood of Christ, and to do this, not in the dark, not at haphazard, not in a world where there is nothing higher than ourselves, but in the "sight of God"—this indeed is an evil more grievous than any other.

If Achab's heart fluttered anxiously when he first saw

The Prophet of Carmel

Elias waiting for him in the road, it sank, as if falling into an icy abyss, as he listened to his message: "Thus saith the Lord: Thou hast slain, moreover thou hast taken possession. Thus saith the Lord: In this place, wherein the dogs have licked the blood of Naboth, they shall lick thy blood also. . . . If Achab die in the city, the dogs shall eat him; but if he die in the field, the birds shall eat him." (3Kng. 21:19,24) The prophet also foretold the utter extermination of his family; and of Jezabel he declared: "The dogs shall eat Jezabel in the field of Jezrahel." (3Kng. 21:23) Such was the tenor of the judgment which Elias had been commissioned by God to announce. The effect upon Achab was sudden and extraordinary. He asked no more irreverent questions. The voice of Elias had prepared the way for the terror of God. Fortunately, Queen Jezabel was at some distance, and unable to soothe him at once with the anodyne of her own diabolical pharmacy. So, "when Achab had heard these words, he rent his garments, and put haircloth upon his flesh, and fasted, and slept in sackcloth, and walked with his head cast down." (3Kng. 21:27) Such was the amazing patience and longsuffering of God, that, as soon as Achab showed signs of repentance, imperfect though it proved to be, He immediately reversed a considerable part of His sentence, a reversal He communicated to Elias, as though He wished not even to exercise His own attribute of forgiveness without justifying the act to him who had been the messenger of His wrath. "The word of the Lord came to Elias the Thesbite, saying, Hast thou not seen Achab humbled before Me? Therefore, because he hath humbled himself for My sake, I will not bring the evil in his days; but in his son's days will I bring the evil upon his house." (3Kng. 21:29)

The Unexpected Meeting

Achab and Elias never met again. The infatuated king, after all his opportunities of grace, put faith in his false prophets, and, against the counsel of Micheas, the prophet of the Lord, went to battle with the Syrians. He disguised himself for safety, but an arrow's shot at a venture wounded him mortally, so that he died in the evening of the battle. "And they buried him in Samaria; and they washed his chariot in the pool of Samaria, and the dogs licked his blood, and they washed the reins, according to the word of the Lord which He had spoken." (3Kng. 22:38)

Let the fate of this king be a lesson to all who call everything good which suits their own desires, and reject the truth as evil if it demands from them a sacrifice. Achab listened willingly to the ministers and mouthpieces of Satan, because "they prophesied good things to the king," and he imprisoned Micheas, and gave him "bread of affliction," because he prophesied evil. (3Kng. 22:27) So it happens perpetually. Men with smooth deference ask advice only in order to appear sincere, or to escape responsibility, or to stifle their uneasy consciences; and then turn like serpents upon their counselor if he opposes them. Lovers of the world hate the doctrine of mortification, although "if ye live according to the flesh, you shall die," says the Apostle. (Rom. 8:13) The seekers after wealth despise the poor, although "there is not a more wicked thing than to love money, for such a one setteth even his own soul to sale. (Eccu. 10:10) They who are devoted to pleasure cannot bear to be warned of their danger, although it is written: "she who liveth in pleasures is dead while she is living." (1Tim. 5:6) Heretics and freethinkers in religion are indignant against the ambassadors of Christ, who reprove, rebuke and exhort, simply because, "according to their own desires, they will heap to themselves teachers, having itching ears;" (2Tim. 5:3) the end of their self-willed theological concupiscence being that they are fatally deceived by the "lying prophets" of their own creation. Achab went to battle only with the Syrians; but when men fight perseveringly against divine truth, and willfully reject that Church who is the sole prophet of God in the world, because she will not be the mouthpiece of their own wishes, their end is something unspeakably worse than the fate of Achab. No archer "shooting at a venture" but the deliberately aimed and unerring arrow of God slays them with the "second death." He hath bent this bow, and made it ready; in it He hath prepared the instruments of death . . . for them that burn." (Ps. 7:13,14) The Samaria in which they are buried is an eternal hell, and the dogs that lick their blood are devils.

The general character of Achab has been clearly manifested in the various parts of his conduct which the sacred narrative has brought before us. What precise amount of the iniquity which he displayed was due to his own spontaneous will, it would be impossible to conjecture. One fact, however, is clear beyond all doubt, and it is too suggestive to be passed by without notice. Disposed to evil as Achab may have been from his early years, that tendency was immensely increased by the influence of his wife. "Now there was not such another as Achab, who was sold to do evil in the sight of the Lord; for his wife Jezabel set him on." (3Kng. 21:25) Whatever may have been the self-chosen perversion of his ideas of right and wrong, whatever may have been the constitutional weakness of his particular temperament, or the force of temptations common to all men as well as to him, there is the authority of revelation for affirming that the most considerable part of his wickedness, the exceptional height to which he grew in crime, was owing to his relations with Jezabel. She, by means of her position in the palace, her opportunities of conversation and of tacit influence through her daily actions, her superior ingenuity, decisiveness of will, malicious energy and the fascinating empire which she had acquired over his affections, quickened, fostered and brought to their fullest maturity all the seeds of evil that were lying in his heart. What he might have been without Jezabel, we cannot say. What he actually became from her example and persuasion, we do know. "There was not such another man as Achab, who was sold to do evil in the sight of the Lord." He committed a great sin in marrying Jezabel, although plausible reasons could no doubt have been alleged in his justification. Jezabel, it might be said, was gifted in person and in mind; she was of royal blood, and in that respect there was equality. The union would lead to a friendly alliance with her father Ethbaal, king of the Sidonians, and that alliance would strengthen Achab's political position, and tend to increase the commercial prosperity of Israel. It would be a wise, patriotic, and popular match. Human nature is not changed. Men will be found even in these days to palliate their crimes and defend them upon grounds which, however plausible, cannot stand the test of examination from a religious point of view. The marriage of Achab became to him the fountain of a continual temptation; it was a proximate occasion of guilt that had neither interruption nor cessation. The words before quoted, "for Jezabel set him on," have not been left on record without a purpose.

One lesson, at all events, which they teach is obvious and practical: the danger of all evil companionship in general, and the serious importance of marriage in particular, as to its bearing upon moral character. Few persons when they contemplate marriage for themselves, or have, as parents or friends, to give advice on this subject to others, realize that fact to its full extent. Man is so constituted by nature that he cannot, however much he might wish it, be a mere isolated unit. We all act and react upon each other; the old upon the young, and the young upon the old; men upon women and women upon men; the good upon the bad and the bad upon the good. Humanity is wonderfully imitative, and almost electrically sensitive to its own currents, intellectual and emotional. The closer and more enduring our contact with each other, the more potent and universal our mutual influence.

If this be so, it is not easy to conceive a combination in which the members are so likely to affect each other for good or evil as that of marriage. Cases exist where husband and wife are ever struggling for independence; where each individuality bristles with distinctiveness and opposition; and where the daily condition of things is a chronic state of war. These, however, are exceptional instances. Where mutual consideration and affection prevail, the ordinary result is that a real, though perhaps unconscious, assimilation goes on, a domestic mesmerizing process, the weaker will following the stronger, so that the "one flesh" becomes synonymous with one character. The married state is one in which the peculiar nature of the bond supplies, encourages and demands manifestations of thought, feeling and conduct which would under a less intimate relationship be much modified, if not entirely suppressed. The tendency of an intercourse so free, so close and so unceasing is to intensify the reciprocal influence of those so united.

If this point were better understood so many marriages would not end in disappointed hopes, unhappy homes or worse. There are marriages whose ultimate effect has been to degrade instead of to elevate the moral and spiritual state of those so joined; marriages which have coarsely checked aspirations formerly high and generous, and have blunted by a slow but sure process a delicacy of conscience that was once a safeguard against evil, and a source of pure self-respect; marriages which have sent weak souls into an unexpected and unprepared arena for conflicts between duty and affection, requiring heroic sanctity in order to endure and conquer. There are marriages, which have led not only to dangerous tepidity in the worship of God but to gross neglect of vital religious obligations towards others — children and servants, for example; marriages also which, by bringing the faithful into intimate contact with heresy, have first diminished their fear of and repugnance to the poison, and finally seduced them into avowed apostasy.

Why are so many marriages disastrous in their moral results? Because, in regard to a matter where religious interests are involved, so much is made of what is convenient and agreeable to the "carnal man," and so little is made of the will of God and the sanctification of souls. Many persons marry without ever praying for light on the subject, or examining themselves to find out if they have any vocation to marry or not. They treat it as a matter with which God has little or nothing to do, either as to rights or providential designs. Few of those who are undoubtedly intended for the matrimonial state determine their choice of a partner with any reference to the effect for good or evil of so serious and intimate a companionship. The pure, for instance, will be found frequently allying themselves with persons attractive in some respects, yet whose career has been marked by licentiousness or other vices. It seems as if all bad habits were supposed to be magically charmed away by the mere fact of marriage, and that a short honeymoon will work a miraculous cure in a character long enslaved in sin. Look at the thoughtlessness, the perilous haste, the giddy capriciousness that is often displayed in deciding upon marriage. One would think that it was a child's toy, that could be broken and tossed aside at pleasure; or a lottery wheel, which, if set in motion, must bring up a prize; or a curious experiment in social philosophy, which might be suspended or abandoned at the first symptom of an unpleasant explosion. On the other hand, look at the long calculation and elaborate scheming that are practised, but under the influence of motives which would hold an exalted place if selfishness were religion. With some persons the chief object is money, so that marriage is to them a thinly disguised commercial transaction, husband and wife constituting the firm. With others, it is a higher rank in society, marriage being the useful ladder for reaching aristocratic fruit not otherwise attainable. But why continue examples? The sad fact to be remembered and deplored is the heedless, mercenary, irreligious spirit in which marriage is frequently regarded by those who profess to believe in its dignity and sacredness.

Christian marriage is a sacrament of the Gospel, symbolizing the ineffable union which the Incarnate God has established between Himself and His Church. It is the consecration of human love to a pure and high purpose, namely, the sanctification of man and the extension of the kingdom of God. It is a bond which, whilst linking two baptized creatures to each other visibly, also joins them invisibly to their Creator and Savior by means of the special grace accompanying that bond. It is a path along which, though chequered with light and shade, the fellow travelers mutually supporting each other are enabled to journey the more easily and securely toward that heavenly Jerusalem where "in the resurrection, they neither marry nor are given in marriage, but are as the angels of God." (Mt. 22:30) Alas! that between marriage as a sacrament and marriage as a life there should be at any time a jarring discord, or that any whose earthly and temporal union typifies another which is divine and eternal should be excluded from the marriage feast of the Lamb, excluded moreover, because of sins which, but for their marriage, would never have been committed.

Chapter Eighteen
The Man of God

Elias Thesbites est.

"... It is Elias, the Thesbite." — 4 Kings 1: 8

From the fierce whirl of the battlefield at Ramoth Galaad, and the Pool of Samaria, in which the gory chariot of the slain Achab was washed — the very dogs, who were the natural scavengers of the city, lapping up the bloodstained water, as they had formerly licked the blood of Achab's victim, the murdered Naboth — we pass to a different scene, the tranquil room of a man grievously ill. Ochozias, the son and successor of Achab, having fallen "through the lattices of his upper chamber," lies on his couch, racked in body with pain, and in mind with anxiety about his chances of recovery. (4Kng. 1:2) Sickness, if severe, probes deeply, not only into the exterior framework, the tissues and nerves of the sufferer, but also into his interior organism. It tears off roughly many a mask hitherto complacently and successfully worn. It crashes through the outer superficial crust of appearances, and brings to light the reality lying beneath. Sickness is a revealing glass, in which often a man sees himself in his true colors for the first time. Health has been both his happiness and his delusion. Just as the inroad of disease draws our attention to the existence, condition and operation of the various wheels of the bodily mechanism, which revolved in health without notice because they worked smoothly and regularly, so, also an analogous process takes place in regard to the invisible world of the soul.

The Prophet of Carmel

When we are at the full tide of bodily health, we are apt to allow the soul to float along without much self-reflection. But sickness is a check and a disturbance. It makes an unexpected pause in our thoughtless career. It forces us into comparative quietness and solitude. It cuts us off from the absorbing bustle of life. The invalid's chamber is for the time a cell of retirement, in which the soul contemplates its actions. The mental pulse is then felt to beat more distinctly than at other times. Sickness, moreover, does not merely assist a person in acquiring a knowledge of the state of his soul, but it frequently exercises a powerful influence upon his whole character. According to his previous moral condition and predominant temperament, it intensifies either his good or his evil qualities and gives a fresh momentum to his inclinations.

Under this kind of trial the bright spots grow into fuller radiance and the dark spots gather increasing blackness. When Job was smitten with "a very grievous ulcer, from the sole of the foot even to the top of his head," he exclaimed with humility: "If we have received good things at the hand of God, why should we not receive evil?" (Job 2:10) And again: "I reprehend myself, and do penance in dust and ashes." (Job 42:6) Whilst in the *Apocalypse* we read of those who "blasphemed the God of heaven because of their pains and wounds, and did not penance from their works." (Apoc. 16:11) As "Ochozias walked in the way of his father and his mother," we shall not be surprised at his conduct.

The spirit of idolatry was strong within him, and having profited nothing by his knowledge of past judgments, he turned in his sickness to Beelzebub, sent messengers, saying to them: "Go, consult Beelzebub, the god of Accaron, whether I shall recover of this my illness." (4Kng. 1:2)

The Man of God

The messengers proceeded on their journey, but before arriving at the shrine of Beelzebub, they were accosted by a stranger, whose countenance was to them unknown, and who gave them a startling and mysterious announcement, without even revealing his name. They were evidently over-powered by his look and tone of sublime authority, for at the risk of their lives, they immediately returned to the king, without fulfilling his commands. The account which they gave was this: "A man met us and said to us, go, and return to the king that sent you, and you shall say to him: Thus saith the Lord: Is it because there was no God in Israel that thou sendest to Beelzebub, the god of Accaron? Therefore, thou shalt not come down from the bed on which thou art gone up, but thou shalt surely die." (4Kng.3:4Ochozias felt instinctively that he had the clue to this alarming interview. He asked: "What manner of man was he who met you and spoke these words?" Worn and languid as he was with his malady, the reply must have struck him with a new pang. "They said: A hairy man, with a girdle of leather about his loins." (4Kng. 7:8) The king had no need to push his inquiries any further. There was but one man to whom the description and language could apply. He said: "It is Elias the Thesbite." He was not dead, then, that inscrutable man; he could still see into the future; and he was as fearless now in denouncing Ochozias as he had been before in denouncing Achab. Kings were as chaff in his sight; he blew their lives away with the breath of his mouth.

Ochozias, although disquieted, was not disconcerted. He determined to send for the prophet. Whether he hoped to bribe him to withdraw the sentence; whether, from curiosity, he wished to see with his own eyes a man whose name must have been associated in his mind with

The Prophet of Carmel

a portentous significance on account of its connection
with his father's and mother's destiny; or whether he
intended to put him to death when he was once in his
power, it is not easy to determine. Whatever may have
been his motive, he sent in search of him a band of fifty
armed soldiers. Elias did not, as on a former occasion,
endeavor to fly; those moments of weakness had passed
away forever. There had been but one short eclipse, and
the sun of his strength shone ever afterwards with uninterrupted splendor. Elias, who was probably at that
time in some part of his favorite Carmel, went up to a
high point of the mountain, and scanned from that natural watchtower the track of his pursuers, as they
wound along from the plain to the rising ground. In
order to show the utter absence of all anxiety, and also
to indicate the authority with which he was invested, he
received them in the attitude of a teacher or a judge.
The captain of the fifty "went up to him, and as he was
sitting on the top of a hill, said to him, 'Man of God, the
king hath commanded that thou come down.'"
(4Kng.1:9) These words were a challenge, and an arrogant insult to Elias. They were directed to him, not as an
individual, but as the acknowledged representative of
God. In the same breath he was addressed as the "man
of God," and yet ordered to attend upon the king as
though he were one of the menials of the royal court.
The person of Elias was the ostensible target, but the
real object assailed was the infinite, invisible God
Himself. Elias, in whose mind and heart the thought and
will of God reigned supreme; Elias, who may almost be
said to have known no other self within him but that
which is indicated by the phrase "man of God," felt at
once the far-reaching and wicked significance of the

king's command. He, "answering, said to the captain of fifty, 'If I be a man of God, let fire come down from heaven, and consume thee and thy fifty.'" (4Kng. 6:10) His reply did not come from himself, but from God. Few were the words he uttered; scarcely had their sound died away when the clouds, hitherto serene, opened; the death-flash issuing from them sprang upon the messengers of Ochozias, and on the armed men who, a moment before, had stood in menacing attitude around the prophet. Nothing was left but a circle of blackened corpses, motionless, hideous. The only living man who remained on the spot and could tell the terrible tale was he who, to vindicate the honor of God, had instantly met an impious presumption by a severe and miraculous chastisement. Elias sat alone amongst the dead, untouched by the fatal fire.

Incredible as it seems, King Ochozias, with that indomitable pertinacity in which the wicked too often surpass the good, sent again another band of soldiers to the prophet. He did what many scientific philosophers would do now in the case of a similar occurrence: attributed the destruction of his messengers to the effect of electricity acting according to its ordinary and inevitable laws, a theory to which the circumstance that the interview with Elias took place upon an exposed eminence might give a plausible confirmation. On the second occasion, the king's command was even more peremptory than on the first. The royal temper had evidently become aroused, and the captain of the fifty thus addressed Elias: "Man of God, thus saith the king, Make haste and come down." (4Kng. 1:11)

The prophet made the same reply as before. With equal promptitude the devouring element came at his bidding,

The Prophet of Carmel

and the captain with his fifty never returned to Ochozias.
Like the first messengers who went to try an issue with the
"man of God," they saw, heard and perished.

Still undeterred by the awful fate of his two armed
bands, reckless of the lives which he had uselessly sacri-
ficed, and more and more irritable from the prolongation
of his sickness, the king sent a third company on the same
errand. At this last interview the fiery death was averted
by the prudence, the humility and the charitable consideration of the captain, as well as by the forbearances of
Elias and the interposition of an angel. The captain on
this occasion does not appear to have delivered the usual
imperious message. He was warned by the past, and
approached Elias in a reverent and suppliant spirit.
"When he was come, he fell upon his knees before Elias,
and besought him, and said: 'Man of God, despise not my
life, and the lives of thy servants that are with me.
Behold! fire came down from heaven and consumed the
two first captains of fifty men, and the fifties that were
with them; but now I beseech thee to spare my life.' And
the angel of the Lord spoke to Elias, saying, 'Go down
with him, fear not.' He, arose, therefore, and went, down
with him to the king." (4Kng. 1:13-15)

Elias was a grand solitary. We read of his being in caves,
in a desert, and on mountaintops; but this was the first
time that he ever set foot within the walls of a palace, and
then his visit was not for his own purposes; it was to ask
no favor, to see no pomp and to enjoy no luxury. He went
by the express command of God to tell with his own lips
what Ochozias refused to believe on the testimony of others: the certainty of his approaching death as a punishment for his idolatrous trust in a false god. "'Because thou
hast sent messengers to consult Beelzebub the god of

The Man of God

Accaron, as though there were no God in Israel of whom thou mightest inquire the word; therefore, from the bed in which thou art gone up thou shalt not come down, but thou shalt surely die.' So he died, according to the word of the Lord which Elias spoke." (4Kng. 1:16,17)

This interview of the prophet with Ochozias was the final act of his public career. He had done with kings, their iniquities and persecutions. Henceforth his remaining days were to be passed in the deep seclusion of what may be termed, without a metaphor, his usual monastic life.

The sin of Ochozias for which he suffered the chastisement of a premature death was his superstitious trust in Beelzebub, "as though there were not a God in Israel" whom he might have consulted, and we perceive something of the same disposition of mind in these more modern days. Men who are ever tossing about from side to side, in the feverish restlessness of their inquiring spirits, will resort to any shrine except the Catholic Church, in which the God of truth perpetually abides. Sometimes their "god of Accaron" is one of those numerous religious sects which repudiate with indignant vehemence the Church's claim of infallibility in teaching the Gospel of Christ, whilst they scruple not to assume the heavy responsibility of condemning that Church out of whose bosom they have originally sprung by the lawless nativity of rebellion. Sometimes the "god" is not the creed even of a community, but merely the individual's private fancy, which sees in the passive letter of the holy scriptures a meaning which is only the changeable reflection of his own fluctuating mind. Nor are there wanting those who attempt to open the gates of the invisible world and, by establishing a fellowship of body and soul with the diabolical inhabitants of a spirit land, endeavor to obtain from them information as to the present and the future. This, if false, is a perilous, as well as a delusive, imposture, and if true, brings with it the poisonous breath of the anathema which clings to all knowledge acquired by violating the commands of God.

There is another form of impiety which surpasses that of Ochozias. Though he ignored the true God, he certainly had not arrived at the conclusion openly avowed and scientifically advocated by some philosophers of this age: that the Creator of the universe is either unwilling or unable to modify, at the humble supplication of His creatures, those physical laws which exist and continue in operation solely by virtue of His infinite power and will. Impiety of this kind recalls to our mind the scoffing question in the book of Job: "Who is the Almighty, that we should serve Him, and what doth it profit us if we pray to Him?" (Job 21:15) These "blind guides" are "scoffers, speaking proud things." (Jude 5:18) They regard the instincts, traditions and beliefs of the human race, barbaric or civilized (to say nothing of the Jewish and Christian revelations), as a "vulgar error," and may be truly said to "meet with darkness in the day, and to grope at noonday as in the night." (Job 5:14)

The case of Ochozias suggests to us another phase of development in impiety which has recently found zealous advocates in certain pages of our periodical literature. Ochozias doubtless suffered many a sharp pain, after he had "fallen through the lattices of his upper chamber," and passed many a weary night; but we do not read that when he knew from Elias the certainty of his impending death, he thought it an act of generosity to his own bruised frame, and to his attendants, to anticipate the inevitable event by an altruistic suicide. The king of Israel did not, in order to shorten the penance of a lingering journey to the royal sepulchre, cut prematurely the "silver cord" (Eccl. 12:6) with his jeweled sword; nor, drinking a potent narcotic mingled conveniently in the wine of his festal goblet, sleep himself comfortably away into eternity without a tremor on his lips or a qualm of his conscience. If there be any fundamental and plain truths that, like vital axioms, ought, without exception, to guide the conduct of man, they are the following: We have not been created at hazard, but according to the decree of infinite Wisdom, upon an immutable plan and for a definite purpose, the manifestation of the glory of God, and the possession of our final beatitude. We are "not our own," but "servants" of our Master, "bought with a great price." Our mortal life is a precious talent committed to our keeping, a sacred deposit for whose proper use in all the details of thought, word and action we shall have to give a strict account to our Judge. Every moment of this existence, an existence depending on the continued union of our soul with our body, has real relations to merit and demerit, extending into great issues beyond the limits of this world and the present time. Suffering is not to be always shunned as an unmixed evil, but on the contrary it is a special means of producing conformity to our crucified Redeemer; (Phil. 2:5,8) of "perfecting the work of patience;" (Jam. 1:4) and of furthering the attainment of a glorious resurrection. (Phil. 3:10,11) Yet, to the shame of humanity, of this age and of our own country, we find persons with cultivated intellects and a professed love of their neighbor's good deliberately rejecting these elementary truths of the natural and revealed law, and in the face of Christendom not only vindicating the morality of self-murder upon principle, but even assigning to it, under certain conditions, an honorable niche in the temple of the social virtues!

Chapter Nineteen
The Parting and Ascension

. . . Ecce currus igneus, et equi ignei diviserunt utrumque; et ascendit Elias per turbinem in caelum.

". . . behold a fiery chariot, and fiery horses parted them both
asunder: and Elias went up by a whirlwind into Heaven."
— 4 Kings 2:11

In tracing the wonderful events of the prophet's history,
we have more than once called attention to the exquisite
tenderness of his character, a trait which is apt to be
overlooked, not on account either of the rarity or the
indistinctness of its manifestations, but because of the
colossal grandeur and startling nature of the chief inci-
dents of his life.

Our imagination is so preoccupied, and we are so dazed
and borne aloft by the sublimities of the prophet, that we
are apt to forget or, at all events, not fully appreciate the
gentleness and tender consideration of the man. When we
look up at some majestic tree, the king of the forest,
which, lifting up its massive trunk and stretching far and
wide its huge arms, towers gigantically above all its fel-
lows, we may easily, in our admiration of its size, fail to
observe with due attention the gracefulness of its form, or
the finely organized structure and varied tints of its
leaves. We have had instances of the tenderness of Elias;
but never perhaps did it appear in so touching a phase as
just before his departure from this earth. Being, as he
was, in immediate expectation of that stupendous event,
and on the point of entering a new and mysterious region,
it might naturally have been conjectured that he would
have been absorbed in the one thought which must have
been deepening and expanding at every moment as the

time for his departure approached the thought of the new and unspeakable realities upon which both his bodily and mental eyes were soon to gaze.

But everything about Elias was out of the common order. From first to last he was an example of sublime surprises, no less in his character than in his miracles. In the full ardor of his yearning to leave a world which had indeed been to him a toilsome place of abode; in the midst of the certain anticipation of speedy rest and joys hitherto unexperienced, he did not forget to think of and care feelingly for others. He knew that his departure, although a gain beyond all comprehension to himself, would be an irreparable loss to his faithful disciple, Eliseus. From the time of their first meeting up to the period when they were about to separate, we have no account of the details of their intercourse. But judging from the character of Elias and the eagerness with which Eliseus followed him, after bidding farewell to his father and mother, it is easy to conclude that nature and grace had combined to unite their hearts in a bond of pure and exalted sympathy worthy both of themselves and of their mutual relations towards God.

Elias seems to have desired to withdraw himself from all human witnesses. The spirit of solitude and humility was strong upon him to the last, but Eliseus clung to him with a boldness and an unflagging perseverance that would take no denial. With the jealous vigilance of a true lover, he promptly resisted every suggestion that implied any separation, however brief, until the hour for the inevitable final parting had arrived. The more Elias endeavored to persuade him to stay behind, the more earnestly did Eliseus reiterate his determination to keep close to his master's side. There was a noble and affecting rivalry of love between them. This was the only contest in which they had ever shown the semblance of variance; and their apparent variance was, in itself, but a fresh sign of their deep concord and an additional pledge of their attachment. Elias and Eliseus were going from Galgal towards Bethel, and Elias said to Eliseus: "Stay thou here, because the Lord hath sent me as far as Bethel"; and Eliseus said to him: "As the Lord liveth, and as thy soul liveth, I will not leave thee" (4Kng. 2:2)

Bethel was one of those few favored cities which, besides other memorable associations clustering round its past history, was at that period sanctified by being the dwelling place of the sons of the prophets, holy communities of men devoted to religious contemplation and study. We can imagine how quickly the news of the approach of two such eminent servants of God would spread, and with what eager reverence all the members of the community would hasten to do them honor. The interest, however, on this occasion was such as could never have been experienced before. It thrilled them with mixed feelings of sadness, curiosity and awe; for by some revelation, the time, nature and extent of which are not recorded, they were aware that Elias was soon about to leave them in a supernatural way. "The sons of the prophets that were at Bethel came forth to Eliseus, and said to him, 'Dost thou know that this day the Lord will take thy master from thee'?" (4Kng. 2:3)

How natural and characteristic was the question! How briefly, yet how clearly, it proved their deep sympathy with Eliseus! They did not say, "Dost thou know that the Lord will this day take Elias away — away from us, or from Israel, or from this world," but "away from thee." The presence of Eliseus before their eyes evidently brought home to them forcibly the great loss which he personally was about to undergo. Eliseus understood them well, for love is an acute interpreter of love. Nevertheless, the question probed him to the quick, and his reply was short and decisive almost to abruptness: "I also know it; hold your peace." (4Kng. 2:3)

The expression, "hold your peace," was not meant as a complaint, still less as a rebuke. It was only a sign that Eliseus shrank from making the impending event, to which the sons of the prophets had alluded, a subject for further inquiry and conversation. Even for the sons of the prophets to speak of it seemed like venturing before the time within the clouds of a great mystery. Moreover, though Eliseus was preparing himself for a loss which would be indescribably severe, he had no desire to have that trial intensified without necessity. There are sorrows over which it is unwise to brood prematurely by a needless anticipation, and which, when they do arrive, are most easily borne in silence. It is best to veil them, as we reverently cover up the dead. Even when friends mention them in order to show their sympathy, the effect is sometimes more painful than soothing. Words of well-intentioned condolence can pierce like a lance, because the original wound is thus brought again and again before the mind. It is opened afresh in the attempted dressing. It is multiplied by being reflected in many mirrors, until the sufferer is inclined to exclaim with Eliseus, "I also know it; hold your peace."

At Bethel the same remarkable dialogue that had taken place between Elias and Eliseus when they quitted Galgal was repeated, and with the same result, a victory for Eliseus: "As the Lord liveth, and thy soul liveth, I will not leave thee." From Bethel they went to Jericho, and there also the sons of the prophets, acting manifestly under the influence of the same feelings and illuminated by the same

The Parting and Ascension

revelation as those at Bethel, addressed Eliseus in precisely identical words: "Dost thou know that this day the Lord will take away thy master from thee?" And again he answered: "I also know it; hold your peace." At Jericho, Elias made another appeal to Eliseus: "Stay here, because the Lord hath sent me as far as Jordan," and Eliseus again refused. This was the last attempt to persuade his faithful minister to leave him. As long as they were permitted to be on the same globe, Eliseus was resolved that nothing should divide them, so "they two went on together." (4Kng. 2:4-6)

"Fifty men, sons of the prophets," watched them with anxious gaze. Following at a distance, they moved forward like men who were drawn irresistibly by some overpowering attraction, and yet feared at every step to advance too quickly or to approach too close. (4Kng. 2:7) They saw the two, upon whom their every thought and every look with breathless intensity was fixed, taking the direction of the familiar Jordan. After following for some time its winding course, they came to a spot where, for a few moments, they paused, as if absorbed in contemplation. Then something waved in the air, and the sons of the prophets perceived that it was the folded mantle[1] of Elias, with which, standing on the reedy bank, and uplifting his hands, he smote the river. In an instant the onward movement of the current ceased, and the checked waters began to range themselves with marvelous precision, as if some angelic hand were invisibly fashioning them into symmetrical order. The hoarse dashing of the stream, agitated by

[1] This mantle of Elias is symbolic of his double spirit granted to the prayer of Eliseus, and by this latter transmitted to the whole order of Carmel, which glories in still possessing the twofold spirit of its leader and founder — the spirit of prayer and of zeal. (Editor's note.)

The Prophet of Carmel

the sudden interruption of its flow, subsided into stillness and two liquid walls rose up and stood fronting each other in silence, motionless, erect, self-poised in perfect balance, yet firmly compact, like solid crystal which some superhuman sword had riven at a single stroke widely asunder. And between them Elias and Eliseus fearlessly walked, the river's uncovered bed forming a triumphal pathway for their feet. "The waters divided hither and thither, and they both passed over on dry ground." (4Kng. 2:8)

On reaching the other side, the first words that were uttered by Elias referred to Eliseus and not to himself. They showed in a most striking manner how, on the very threshold of his own exaltation and glory, he wished to obtain for his companion such a gift as would turn their last farewell into an extraordinary blessing and honor. "Ask of me," he said, "what thou wilt have me to do for thee, before I be taken away from thee." And Eliseus said: "I beseech thee that in me may be thy double spirit."[2]

This answer of Eliseus, whilst it expressed an immense faith in the power of Elias with God, revealed also his own sublime ambition. He asked for nothing earthly, for no exemption from persecution or labor, not even for special consolation and strength in his hour of bereavement and loneliness. All he longed for was that he, the servant, might be made like his master; that he, the miraculously adopted firstborn and only son, might be worthy of such a father; and that, if possible, he might not only become his true successor in the prophetical office, but also the complete heir of his spirit to the fullest extent — the spirit of zeal, mortification, miraculous power, intellectual illumi-

[2] In allusion, probably, to the law by which the first-born received a double portion of the father's inheritance. (Deut. 21:17)

The Parting and Ascension

nation and pure ardor of the affections, as manifested both in the active and the contemplative life. Eliseus, knowing the immense task that would devolve upon him after the removal of his spiritual father, craved humbly for a grace sufficient for his ministry and so preeminent above that of ordinary prophets, that his title to be the future representative of Elias would be self-evident to all Israel. Elias answered: "Thou hast asked a hard thing; nevertheless, if thou see me when I am taken from thee, thou shalt have what thou hast asked; but if thou see me not, thou shalt not have it." (4Kng. 2:10)

Every instant now became more precious. Who can attempt to imagine the feelings of Elias and Eliseus? They did not remain silent. Their minds were too full of many and deep thoughts, and their hearts were stirred by emotions too strong for silence. The mutual currents of their pure and grand souls intermingled more closely at every step as "they went on walking and talking together"; and then, apparently without any premonitory sign, whilst voice was answering voice, and look was answering look, "behold, a fiery chariot and fiery horses parted them both asunder; and Elias went up by a whirlwind into heaven." (4Kng. 2:11)

Amidst the dazzling light of a flood of splendor scarcely endurable by mortal eye, amidst the rush and roar of the mighty blast, as it swept far and wide around the celestial chariot and its unearthly coursers, Eliseus stood undismayed. As he fixed his eager gaze upon the tremendous scene, an exclamation, expressive at once of wonder, joy and loving sadness, burst forth from his lips: "My father, my father, the chariot of Israel and the driver thereof." (4Kng. 2:12)

The Prophet of Carmel

This was the only farewell, the only embrace, the only outward sign of reverence and love that he could give. His heart was too full to say much and, even had it been able, the words would have found no listener present. "My father, my father, the chariot of Israel and the driver thereof!" Eliseus felt that not only was he himself now bereft of a father, but the whole of Israel also. Little had Elias been honored and followed by that sensual, fickle and ungrateful people; nevertheless, he had ever been their divine guide, and their true witness against falsehood, immorality and apostasy. He had ever been that patient, persevering intercessor with God whose prayers were more powerful than all their military array, the fearless and uncompromising warrior of the Lord, the very personification of spiritual force and rapidity combined. Not a driver without a chariot, nor a chariot without a driver, but both together, united in one individual. And so extraordinary had he been in his life and mission, so unequaled in the majestic singularity of his excellence, so exalted above all others who were in any way a moral power for good in Israel, that Eliseus called him "the chariot and driver thereof," as if to indicate that Israel had but one chariot and one driver, and that Elias was his name.

Tender and piercing was the cry of Eliseus, but no answer came back. The "fiery chariot and fiery horses" had gone, and not a trace of their marvelous pathway could be any longer discerned. At first the great vision must have seemed too intensely real and glorious to be able to wane or vanish away so quickly, but when Eliseus had uttered his few words and given his rapid glance, all was ended. Elias had disappeared, and "he saw him no more." He saw the heavens above, through whose golden gates the ascending prophet had just passed in triumph.

The Parting and Ascension

He saw the ancient Jordan flowing peacefully near him, and the sons of the prophets watching still in the distance; and the well-known mantle[11] lying, like a suddenly revealed treasure, at his feet, for there that precious relic, full of august memories and wonder-working virtue, had fallen. But in vain did his keen eyes scan far and wide the clear and vast expanse of that eastern sky in search of Elias himself.

We can scarcely reflect on the translation of Elias without contrasting it with the ascension of Him of whom Elias is the figure and the future precursor. As Elias was taken up in the sight of the sons of the prophets whilst conversing with the beloved Eliseus, his divinely appointed successor, so Jesus passed His last moments upon the earth in instructing and consoling those whom He intended to leave behind Him as the vicarious ministers of His kingdom. "He that heareth you heareth Me." "The Lord Jesus after He had spoken to them was taken up into heaven." (Mk. 16:9) "While they looked on, He was raised up, and a cloud received Him out of their sight." (Acts 1:9) As soon as He had gone, two angels "in white garments" assured the disciples, as St. Chrysostom says, of His visible return again from heaven in clouds of glory, lest they might imagine that He had departed, like Elias, not into the true heaven, but into some inferior place. "Elias was indeed taken up as if into heaven, for he was a servant; Jesus, however, into heaven itself, because He was the Lord; the one went up in a fiery chariot, the other in a cloud. When it was necessary for the servant to be summoned, a chariot was sent for him; but when the Son was to depart, a royal throne was ready, and not that merely, but even the very Father's throne itself. Isaias says, 'Behold, the Lord sitteth upon a cloud. . .' (Isa. 19:1); therefore, He sends a cloud for His

The Prophet of Carmel

Son. Elias, when ascending, let a sheepskin mantle fall upon Eliseus; but Jesus, when ascending, sent down gifts of graces upon the disciples, not in order to make one prophet only, but an infinite number of prophets, greater and more illustrious than Eliseus."[3]

Elias, as St. Gregory observes, "was carried up by angels in a chariot, in order to demonstrate openly that he, being a mere man, required the assistance of others, because he, whom the inferiority of his nature weighed down, could not rise by his own strength even into the aerial heaven. But we do not read that our Redeemer was lifted up in a chariot by angels. He, indeed, who made all things, was carried above all things by His own power. He returned to the place where He already was: and He remained in the place which He had left; because, though He ascended by His humanity into heaven, yet He encompassed equally heaven and earth by His Godhead."[4]

The ascension of Elias is alluded to by St. Ambrose, with a beautiful quaintness, in his commentary on the words "chariots of Aminadab," in the *Canticle of Canticles*. (Cant.6:11) He describes the soul of man under the allegory of a chariot which has either good or bad horses. The four good steeds are prudence, temperance, fortitude and justice; the four bad steeds are anger, concupiscence, fear, injustice. The bad horses are often at issue with themselves; sometimes anger stretches forward too far and fear pulls back to excess, so as to imperil the chariot. The good horses, on the contrary, spring forward rapidly, as if winged, from earthly to heavenly regions, and lift up the soul on high, especially

[3] St. Chrysos. Hom, in Asc. D. N. J. C., Sect. 5. Hom.,

[4] St. Greg. Hom., xix, in Evang.

184

The Parting and Ascension

if they bear that sweet yoke of which it is said, "My yoke is sweet and My burden is light."[5]

As Eliseus saw nothing more of Elias after his ascension, so we also have now taken our last look at the great prophet, for in the pages of the Old Testament we behold him no more.

But though the prophet's biography is ended and he has now passed out of our view, yet, as his form and appearance as he arose from the earth were indelibly impressed upon the memory of Eliseus, so also should his image be often stamped by meditation upon our minds. We shall indeed have read in vain the inspired account of Elias unless we rise from its perusal, not merely with our imagination glowing ardently with the singularly fascinating interest excited by his career, but also with an earnest resolution to keep him frequently in our thoughts. There is much in his history upon which we can only look with a wonder excluding the very idea of imitation. Still, as we have seen, there is also much from which we can derive lessons.

To admit the attractiveness of the history which we have been considering, and allow it to lie outside the soul; to have, like Moses, "seen a great sight," and then to walk away without receiving any new illumination and fire into our hearts — this would surely be a grave neglect of an opportunity of grace.

The true history of any saint, still more an inspired history, is a kind of a reflected presence of the saint himself. They who read his life should strive, according to their measure and graces, to imitate it. To read about the saints without any object but a temporary gratification of the intellect, is to treat their memory with disrespect.

[5] St. Ambrose: De Isaac et Anima, 77. and Mt. 9:30.

The Prophet of Carmel

When Eliseus knew that Elias had departed, he did not remain any longer on the spot, gazing curiously and uselessly upwards. He did not speculate or brood idly over his altered position: his solitude, for instance, in the absence of Elias, his immense responsibility as his successor, or the uncertainty of the future prospects of Israel. After rending his garments, to give vent to his deep emotion, and perhaps also to signify that a new Eliseus was henceforth to rise up out of the old, he instantly began to act "in the spirit and power of Elias." "He took up the mantle of Elias that fell from him, and going back, he stood upon the bank of the Jordan; and he struck the waters with the mantle of Elias that had fallen from him; and they were not divided." Eliseus, however, was a man of faith and perseverance. Failing the first time, he tried again. He said: "Where is now the God of Elias? And he struck the waters, and they were divided hither and thither, and Eliseus passed over." (4Kng. 2:13,14)

So let it be with ourselves. Rending in pieces and casting off the former garments of our imperfections and sins, let us "take up the mantle of Elias." To do this, we must strive to clothe ourselves with the spirit of his character, that spirit which manifested itself in his consuming zeal; his dauntless courage before hostile kings and excited multitudes; his outspoken indignation against iniquity; his mortification, preeminently conspicuous in his dress, food and dwelling-places; his angelic purity and promptitude in obeying the "word of the Lord" whenever and wherever he heard its voice; his tender sympathy for the bereaved and sorrowful, as Sarephta will ever testify; and the depth, fidelity and delicacy of his human friendship, as we have seen evidenced in his relations with Eliseus. If we are clad in this mantle, hard and painful though it may appear to self-indulgent souls (just as the rough sheepskin of Elias would have been to effeminate bodies) we carry with us an irresistible power.

We, like Eliseus, have our Jordan to cross, or rather, not one but many: temptations to evil, trials to be endured at the hands of foes and sometimes even of friends, struggles of mind and weaknesses of body, the monotony and labor of life, faults to be corrected, and virtuous habits to be acquired, strengthened and confirmed — what are these but so many Jordans in our path which we must attempt to cross, and in which many are lost without a recovery? Elias and Eliseus, "in order that they might pass over the waters of the Jordan, had first walked over the streams of the passions with their mind!"[6]

If, however, according to our measure and opportunity, we bear upon our souls the spiritual mantle of the Thesbite, we need fear no evil. Not only is his God our God also, but we have, under the New Dispensation, "better things" than he could possibly possess.

Instead of that "little cloud like a man's foot," which, floating up from the Mediterranean, was symbolic of the future humanity of Christ, has not the shadow been succeeded by the reality, the resemblance to a man's foot by the Son of Man Himself? Has not the Word been made Flesh, rising from the ocean of divine love into this visible world by His nativity; from the sealed sepulchre into the triumphant liberty of a new and impassible life by His resurrection; and from earth to heaven by His glorious ascension? The appearance of the cloud coming up from the sea was followed, in answer to the prophet's prayer, by a temporal blessing only: "There fell a great rain." But Christ was born, suffered and died, rose again, and went up into the

[6] St. Ambrose, in Ps. cxviii, 16.

heavens, that He might send down upon us the sevenfold gifts of the Spirit, even the Holy Ghost Himself, for our sanctification and salvation. "If I go not, the Paraclete will not come to you; but if I go, I will send Him to you." (Jn. 16:7)

Has not the broken altar on Mount Carmel, which was repaired with "twelve stones, according to the number of the twelve tribes of Jacob," been succeeded by one upon which no bullock "cut to pieces" lies, but that "Lamb of God Who taketh away the sin of the world," (Jn.1:29) an "altar whereof they have no power to eat who serve the tabernacle," (Heb.13:10) an altar around which gather not the people of one small nation, but of all the earth, to feed upon the "Bread which cometh down from heaven," and "of which if any man eat, he shall live for ever?" (Jn.6:50,52)

A voice from God spoke to Elias, when he was on the threshold of the cave at Horeb; but are not we far more than listeners to an audible sound, being "partakers of the divine nature," (2Pet. 1:4) and "children of God," (Gal. 3:23) begotten of the Father of Lights "by the Word of Truth?" (Jam. 1:17,18)

Has not Horeb, with its "strong wind overthrowing the mountains," its earthquakes and fire, and its "whistling of a gentle air," been followed by the marvelous breathing, light and presence of the Holy Ghost, a presence not transient or external, like the brief duration of the prophet's vision, but indwelling and perpetual in the Catholic Church? "I will ask the Father, and He shall give you another Paraclete, that He may abide with you for ever; the Spirit of Truth, whom the world cannot receive, because it seeth Him not, nor knoweth Him; but you shall know Him, because He shall abide with you and be in you." (Jn. 14:16,17) "Know you not that your members are the temple of the Holy Ghost, who is in you, whom you have from God?" (1Cor. 6:19) "You are fellow citizens with the saints, and the domestics of God, built upon the foundation of the Apostles and prophets, Jesus Christ Himself being the chief cornerstone, in whom all the building being fitly framed together groweth up into a holy temple in the Lord, in whom you also are built together into a habitation of God in the Spirit." (Eph. 2:19-22) "We all, beholding the glory of the Lord with open face, are transformed into the same image from glory to glory, as by the Spirit of the Lord." (2Cor. 3:18)

If Elias, braving the tempest, outstripped the fleet chariot of Achab, because "the hand of the Lord was upon him," imparting to his limbs a preternatural strength and speed, do we not run in a race far more perilous: a race that must be run in the storm of evil passions and the ceaseless downpour of temptation and difficulties; a race, not extending over a short space only, as from Carmel to Jezrahel, but continuing from the cradle to the grave? Yet in this tremendous race why need we fail? We can do all things in Him who strengtheneth us. We can "run not as uncertainly" but "so as to obtain" that prize, which "the just Judge will render to them that love His coming:" the "crown of justice, the crown of life, the crown of glory." (2Tim. 4:8)Why should we be afraid or cast down? "We know whom we have trusted."

If, then, we find ourselves in the presence of difficulties which appear, and really are, insurmountable to mere human strength, let us cry out like Eliseus, confidently and perseveringly, "Where is now the God of Elias?" and assuredly we will be heard. Every Jordan, no matter how broad, or deep, or tortuous, or rapid, will be safely crossed; and our journey in this land of exile being ended, we need not be dismayed when we come to that last river, the river of death, upon whose mysterious waters even the bravest and holiest cannot look without instinctive awe. The momentous stream will be "divided hither and thither," and we shall pass over victoriously; from tremulous hope to blissful certainty; from perpetual danger to everlasting security; from a world of snares, toil and sorrows, to those "green pastures and still waters" which can be found only on the other side, and whose final possession is as certain as the truth, mercy and existence of God Himself. "For God is faithful" and "this is the promise which He hath promised us — life everlasting." (1Jn. 2:25)

Appendix

Although these topics are beyond the range of the history of Elias in the Old Testament, the special subject of this volume, some observations upon them, drawn from approved theological sources, will form a supplement not unacceptable to the reader.

1. The condition and abode of Elias after his translation.

Suarez, who in his *Mysteria Vitae Christi* treats of the first three questions with his usual exhaustive fullness, minute accuracy and luminous subtlety, says, "It is of faith" that neither Henoch nor Elias have ever died. Holy scripture is explicit on the point. "Henoch walked with God, and was seen no more, because God took him." (Gen. 5:22) In the same chapter all the other patriarchs, from Adam to Lamech, are enumerated, and it is declared of all but Henoch that they "died," an exception full of significance. "Henoch pleased God, and was translated into Paradise, that he may give repentance to the nations." (Eccu.44:16) He will not, therefore, die until he has fulfilled that duty. "Henoch was translated that he should not see death, and he was not found because God had translated him." (Heb.11:5) Of Elias it is declared that he was taken up in a whirlwind of fire, in a chariot of fiery horses, and is registered ("who art registered") "in the judgments of times,

to appease the wrath of the Lord, to reconcile the heart of
the father to the son, and to restore the tribes of Jacob."[1]
By being "registered in the judgments of times" is to be
understood that he is destined, at some future period
already fixed by the divine decree, to "appease the wrath
of the Lord." Compare these last words with Malachi 5:6,
vi, where it is said: "Behold, I send you Elias the prophet
before the coming of the great and dreadful day of the
Lord, and he shall turn the heart of the fathers to the children, and the heart of the children to the fathers; lest I
come (i.e., that I may not come) and strike the earth with
anathema." "Neither Henoch nor Elias," says St.
Augustine, "has withered into corruption through so long
an old age."[2] "Henoch and Elias," says St. Jerome, "have
the same limbs now which they possessed when they were
translated."[3] "Elias has not evaded death, but put it off."[4]
"Elias, who preserved virginity from his birth, has been
carried into heaven; . . . he survives to this time."[5]

Since Henoch and Elias are not dead, but live in their
original bodies, a question arises as to their corporal condition. How, for instance, are they preserved from death?
St. Epiphanius considers that they "live in a spiritual and
not in an animal fashion, and are nourished upon some
spiritual aliment, of which God is the supplier, who knows
things hidden and created things invisible."[6] St. Augustine
says that "if they do not require food they are sustained as
was Elias during his fast of forty days on his way to Horeb;
or that if they do need food, they live, perhaps, in

[1] De Peccatorum Meritis, c. iii.
[2] Ep. lxi ad Pammachium.
[3] St. Greg. lib. ii, Hom. in Evang.,xxix, s. 5.
[4] St. Epiphan. Haer. lib. iii, lix, al. lxxix.
[5] St. Epiphan. Haer. lib., iii, xliv, al. lxiv, 5.

Appendix

Paradise like Adam before his expulsion, who was preserved from wasting away (*defectio*) by eating of the fruits
of the garden; and from old age by eating of the tree of life.
Habebat enim (quantum existimo) et de lignorum fructibus
refectionem contra defectionem, et de ligno vitae stabil: tatem
contra vetustatem."[6] St. Thomas states distinctly that
Henoch and Elias fed often upon the fruit of the tree of life
from the time of their translation to paradise, and also
that in consequence of such nourishment their bodies
became solidified (*solidata*), and will not be corrupted
after their death at the end of the world.[7]

Are the bodies of Henoch and Elias in a glorified condition? This depends, says Suarez,[8] upon another question—
whether their souls are glorified. As the state of the body
follows that of the soul, then if the latter be not glorified,
neither will be the former. Their souls are not glorified, (1)
because they have to die, and it was the peculiar privilege of
Christ alone that He possessed the beatific vision in His soul
whilst still living in a mortal body; (2) because if their souls
were glorified, then must their bodies have also shared in
that glory; but the death which they are destined to undergo hereafter would necessarily interrupt the immortality of
the body, and subject it to pain and separation from the
soul, a state inconsistent with that of the true glory of the
bodies of the just, which, once bestowed, can never be lost.
Hence St. Augustine says, "I do not believe that they" (i.e.,
Henoch and Elias) "have been changed into that spiritual
quality of body which is promised in the resurrection, and
of which the first example is to be found in the Lord."[9]

[6] De Pecc. Mer. c. iii.
[7] Comm. in Apocal. xi, 8, s. 1, f.
[8] Myst. Vit. Christi, q. lix, disp. Iv, sec. 1.
[9] De Pecc. Mer. c. iii.

The Prophet of Carmel

Tertullian says that Henoch and Elias, because they have not yet died and have not reached their full term by a resurrection, are by that very fact candidates at the present day (*hodie*) for eternity, and are thoroughly experiencing (*ediscunt*) immunity of the flesh from every vice, from every loss, from every injury, and from every dishonorable treatment.[10]

If it be alleged that Elias must be enjoying the vision of God, or else it would be wrong to commemorate him by a festival,[11] and to dedicate churches to his name, the answer is that the objection is invalid, because the institution of a festival or the dedication of a church does not necessarily imply anything more than a solemn recognition of the virtues of the saints thus honored, or some special fact in their history redounding to their glory. Temples are not dedicated, strictly speaking, to the saints themselves, but to *God alone*, in honor of the saints.[12]

Though Henoch and Elias do not enjoy the clear vision of God, they, however, possess an extraordinary power of divine contemplation and love, in which exercise they are unceasingly engaged; for they are perfectly free from any irregular movements that could disturb their souls, and from any corporal impediment, such as is alluded to in *Wisdom*: "The corruptible body is a load upon the soul, and the earthly habitation presseth down the mind, which museth upon many things."[13] "Happy manifestly are

[10] De Resurrec. Carnis, 58.

[11] Off. Carm. Disc. 20 Julii, & Martyrol. Rom.

[12] Cornel. a Lapide, Comm. in Gen. c. v. 24, where he treats at some length the question of "suspension of merits." In reference to the intention of the Church in dedicating temples and altars to the saints, see Trombelli, De B. Mariae Vita, p. 11. Diss. xix. s. 3; and for the cultus of Elias, the Acta Sanctorum, De St. Elia, xx. Julii.

[13] Wis. 4:15.

Appendix

Henoch taken away and Elias translated, for they live to God alone, and are occupied in Him alone, by understanding, loving and enjoying Him."[14B] "I conclude," says Suarez, "that they have the delight of receiving immense consolations from God, divine illuminations and frequent revelations, at all events about those matters which are suitable to their condition. I doubt not that they knew of the coming of Christ and the completion of the world's redemption by Him; because they had beforehand an explicit belief in His advent, for which also they had ardently yearned, and it was unbecoming that they should be left now in darkness and error. With regard to Elias, it is clear from the Gospel that he saw Christ at the Transfiguration, and we may presume that Henoch also has at some period beheld Him. But whether they now see Him, at least in His humanity, is uncertain."[15] That they were confirmed in grace at their translation and are, therefore, incapable of sinning, is only a reasonable conclusion. If they cannot merit, neither can they justly be liable to demerit, a danger which, if possible, would also impair their happiness.

In answer to the question whether Henoch and Elias are capable, in their existent state, of acquiring merit, since they are not dead and are not enrolled among the saints who have fulfilled their time of probation, Suarez, with the majority of theologians, replies in the negative. The chief argument for the affirmative rests on the fact that they are still walking by faith, and on the supposition that they are suffering intense pain from their solitude, and above all, from their privation of the vision of God, without reaping from that loss any advantage to themselves.

[14] St. Bern., Ser. vi, in Asc. Dom.
[15] Myst. v. Christi, loc. cit.

The Prophet of Carmel

Suarez answers, (1) that ordinarily God has determined that a man's capacity for meriting is terminated by his death; and that in the case of Henoch and Elias their removal from the present scene of human action is analogous to death, so far as merit is concerned; (2) that they bear their exile with pleasure, on account of their charity and conformity to the divine will; (3) that they knew when they were being taken up from this world that they would have a long period to wait, and by their perfect obedience to this decree they merited much; and (4) that as they will return to the world and suffer for Christ, they will thus obtain an increase of merit and glory far beyond the detriment incurred from a temporary delay of the beatific vision. Thus their power of merit is not finally terminated, but only suspended until they come again to labor and to die. If their merits were to go on accumulating until the end of the world, they would exceed, says the same author— not only those of other saints, but of the Blessed Virgin herself.*

It is natural to ask where Henoch and Elias are dwelling, since they are not as yet admitted into the heaven of the "spirits of the just made perfect."[16] Most of the fathers believe that they were elevated first into the aerial, as distinguished from the ethereal, heaven and then were transferred to a terrestrial paradise, either the original Eden of our first parents, or one specially prepared

*Editor's note: On this point the editors disagree with Suarez. Our Lady's veneration has a unique rank which the Church titles hyperdulia, whereas all the other saints are granted the *cultus of dulia*. Only God is worshiped with the cultus of latria, which is, of course, supreme adoration. It is the common opinion of all the saints who lived after the Council of Trent, that the merits of the Mother of God exceed that of all angels and saints combined.

[16] Heb.7:23.

Appendix

for them by God. St. Gregory explains the aerial heaven to be that which is close to the earth. It is the heaven in which birds fly, whence they are called "birds of heaven," (*volucres coeli*);[17] and he says that "Elias was carried up into this heaven, in order that he might be suddenly conveyed to some secret region of the earth, where he might live in great repose of the spirit and the flesh, until he shall return at the end of the world and pay the debt of death."[18] With this opinion St. Thomas agrees. "Elias was raised into the aerial, not the empyrean, heaven which is the abode of the saints, and in like manner Henoch was carried away to a terrestrial paradise, where he and Elias, it is believed, will live together until the coming of Antichrist."[19] St. Thomas considers that this Paradise is the Eden of our first parents, which has been preserved for Henoch and Elias.[20] St. Augustine, as we have seen, admits the probability of that opinion. St. Jerome calls Henoch and Elias "settlers (*coloni*) in Paradise."[21] Suarez thinks that Henoch may have lived in the original Paradise until the Deluge and then, after being in some way divinely kept from harm, he was transferred to a hidden spot, which may possibly be on the same site as that Paradise which was destroyed by the waters. Wherever their abode may be, he cannot doubt but that Henoch and Elias are intensely happy in their mutual fellowship, and that they live in a place which, if not the Paradise of Adam and Eve, is equally beautiful. He states, however, that some of the fathers, amongst whom are St. Jerome[22]

[17] Mt.8: 20, Vulg.
[18] Lib. ii, Hom. xxix, in Evang. sec. 5.
[19] ibid. iii, Q. xlix, art. 5, Summae.
[20] ibid. i, Q. cii, art. 2 ad 3.
[21] Ep. 61, ad Pammachium.

and St. Ambrose,[23] believed that they inhabited the ethereal and not the aerial heavens, beyond the region of the earth. "Elias who walked on the earth lives in the heavens with the angels."[24] Theodoret, in allusion to the same event, writes: "These things which have been committed to silence are not to be investigated; but those things which have been written are to be venerated."[25] The Septuagint, in reference to Elias, describes him to have been taken up "as if" into heaven. "There are questions," says St. Augustine, "in regard to which, without any prejudice to that faith by which we are Christians (*salva fide qua Christiani sumus*) either there may be ignorance as to what is the truth, and therefore any definitive judgment is suspended; or, we may make a guess which, on account of our human and frail misgiving (*infirma suspicione*), may be inconsistent with fact; as, for instance, when the question is raised as to the site of the Paradise in which God placed man after forming him from the dust, because the Christian does not doubt of the existence of Paradise; or when it is asked, where Elias and Henoch are at this moment; for we doubt not that they are alive in the bodies in which they were born."[26]

This seems the place to mention a circumstance which has been supposed to prove that Elias, though living out of the world, nevertheless, on one occasion after his translation, sent a message to a king of Juda. Many commentators are of the opinion that Elias knew by some revelation that Joram the son of Josaphat was not walking in the good

[22] Com. in Amos, ix.
[23] De Paradiso, c. iii.
[24] Dorotheus, Synop. ap. Suar.
[25] Q. xlv in Gen.
[26] De Pecc. Orig. xxiii, 27.

Appendix

ways of his father, and wrote a letter threatening him with the infliction of a terrible plague upon his family and his people, and of a loathsome and fatal disease upon himself, unless he repented. "There was a letter brought to him from Elias the prophet."[27] If this letter was given to Joram soon after it had been composed, and if Elias had been translated some time before Joram had succeeded his father in the kingdom, it is evident that Elias must have written the epistle in his preternatural abode, and sent it thence by angelic or other extraordinary agency. Cornelius a Lapide holds this view strongly and quotes several other weighty names in its support. Estius also is of the same opinion. The following interpretations of the passage have also been suggested. (1) Elias may have penned the letter before his translation, by a prophetical anticipation, and left it in the hands of Eliseus to be presented at the most fitting time; and coming from Elias who was well known to have left the visible world, it would no doubt be invested with a very solemn importance.[28] (2) Under the name of Elias it may have been intended to designate Eliseus his successor. Cajetan suggests also that there may have been another prophet, not the Thesbite, called Elias.[29] (3) The order of events may not have been intended to synchronize exactly with the order of the narrative — a custom not uncommon in the biblical writings when it is desired to complete a personal history or to classify a series of sayings without breaking the unity of the matter by a strictly chronological sequence of events. Upon this hypothesis it has been conjectured that Elias lived until the first few years of Joram's reign and, if so, he might of course have

[27] 2 Para.21:12.
[28] Tirinus, Comm. in loc.
[29] Cornelius. a Lapide. op. cit.

sent a letter to him by the hands of Eliseus or some of the "sons of the prophets."

2. The appearance of Elias on the Mount of Transfiguration.

It is a revealed truth that Elias, together with Moses, was present with Christ at His Transfiguration, was seen by Peter, James and John, and was also heard to converse with their Lord. "Behold, there appeared to them Moses and Elias talking with Him."[30] "There appeared to them Elias with Moses, and they were talking with Jesus."[31] "Behold, two men were talking with Him, and they were Moses and Elias."[32] Since Moses was dead, it is impossible to know whether, as some suppose, he resumed for the time his original body, like many who came out of their tombs when Jesus "yielded up the ghost;"[33] or whether he was clothed in a material form supplied to him by divine power;[34] or whether he only presented the optical appearance of a body. Suarez inclines to the opinion that Moses was present in his real body by means of a temporary resurrection in order that he, as well as Elias, might be ocular witnesses of the glory of the Lord, which he could not truly have been if he was not in his own body. This view is most in accordance with the letter of the scripture which describes Moses, Elias and Christ as all present together, without hinting at any such distinction as would imply that Moses was there in a manner different from the true corporeal presence of our Lord and Elias. It also harmonizes

[30] Mt.17:3.
[31] Mk.9: 3.
[32] Lk.9:30.
[33] Mt.27:52.
[34] St. Thom. iii, q. xlv, iii, ad 2.

Appendix

with the belief of many of the fathers that God fulfilled in the Transfiguration the promise which He had made to Moses at Horeb, that "His face should go before him," but that he would not be able then to "behold His face and live,"[35] a promise indicated again in the words, "I speak to him mouth to mouth, and plainly; and not by figures, doth he see the Lord."[36] Suarez cites St. Jerome, St. Cyril of Jerusalem, St. Irenaeus, Tertullian and Origen as favoring the same interpretation.[37] Whatever questions may be raised about Moses, there seems no reason to doubt that Elias was present in his actual, passible body.

To the question, why Moses and Elias were specially chosen to be upon the mount rather than other saints, various answers are given by theologians. St. Chrysostom offers the following explanation: 1) Because, since many of the Jews thought that Christ was Elias or Jeremias, the presence of Elias and Moses as attendants upon Christ would prove the distinction between the servants and the Master. 2) The charge against our Lord of being a violator of the Mosaic Law and a blasphemer was refuted by the attesting presence of the Lawgiver, and of that prophet who had been eminent for zeal in the cause of God. 3) To show that, by bringing up the dead Moses from the grave, and the living Elias from his unknown abode, Christ has power over the living and dead. 4) To fortify the disciples against the fear of death, by bringing before them Moses and Elias conversing calmly about the approaching passion of Christ, these two having set illustrious examples of fearlessness — Moses before Pharaoh, and Elias before Achab. 5) To teach the disci-

[35] Ex.33:13-23.
[36] Num.12:8.
[37] Myst. V. Christi, Q. xlv, art. iv, disp. xxxii, s. 2.

The Prophet of Carmel

The Prophet of Carmel

ples the meekness of Moses and the zeal of Elias, who were at the same time inflexible and careful leaders of the people.[38] So St. Thomas cites the above reasons, together with another from St. Hilary (Can. xvii. in Matt.), namely, that as Moses represented the Law and Elias the prophets, Christ was thus attested to be the Messias by both the Law and the prophets.[39]

Toletus discusses the above reasons, and adds one of his own, which is well worthy of consideration.[40] At the promulgation of the Law on Sinai, the people, being in terrible fear of hearing the voice of God amidst the thunders and lightenings, begged that Moses might receive the commandments instead of themselves. "Thou shalt speak to us, and we will hear and do them."[41] God accepted their proposal: "They have spoken all things well." And then He revealed to them the great prophecy about the future Christ: "I will raise them up a prophet out of the midst of their brethren like unto thee (alluding to Moses) and I will put My words in His mouth, and He shall speak to them all that I shall command Him."[42] What testimony to Christ could be stronger, therefore, than the fact that Moses himself, whom the ancient Israelites had agreed to obey, appeared in person on the mount with Christ, and thus pointed to Him as the Prophet whom God, ages ago, on Sinai, had promised through Moses to send them, and whom, as typically represented by Moses, they had agreed to hear?

Elias was there to bear witness like Moses, but on other grounds. Malachi, four hundred years previously, had

[38] St. Chrysost. Hom. 57 al. 28 in Matt.
[39] St. Thom. iii q. xlv, art. iii, ad 3.
[40] Comm. in ix Luc. Annot. lxiv.
[41] Deut. 5:27.
[42] Deut. 18:18.

202

Appendix

distinctly predicted the coming of Elias as the precursor of the second advent of Christ. "Behold, I will send you Elias the prophet" (in the Septuagint it is "Elias the Thesbite") "before the coming of the great and dreadful day of the Lord."[43] Elias must have known, if anyone did, who He was that stood transfigured between himself and Moses, so "that His face did shine as the sun, and His garments became white as snow."[44] Elias had for about nine hundred years been expecting the coming of Christ, and he knew that he was destined by the decree of God and for the accomplishment of prophecy, to be the forerunner of His return in "the clouds of heaven with much power and majesty."[45] He showed also, by speaking "of His decease that He should accomplish in Jerusalem," that the Christ who was now seen glorified would soon undergo death, not by chance or necessity, but by His own deliberate choice. Thus, under circumstances deeply and supernaturally impressive, for Elias is described, together with Moses, as not only "appearing," but "appearing in majesty,"[46] he testified to the identity of a suffering and dying Jesus with that Son of Man who will come to judge the world at the "great and terrible day of the Lord." By the significant presence of Moses and Elias, the disciples were confirmed in their faith, and taught that the Cross of Christ would end in that glory of which the splendor of the Transfiguration was only a faint presage. "Henoch was not present," observes Toletus, "because he lived before the Law was given to the Jews."

[43] Mal. iv, 5.
[44] Mt. 15:2 2.
[45] Mt. 24:30.
[46] Lk. 9:31.

The Prophet of Carmel

3. The return of Elias in the last days.

Malachi alludes to Elias when he represents God as declaring: "Behold, I will send you Elias the prophet before the coming of the great and terrible day of the Lord."[47] Jesus Christ confirms this interpretation by His answer to His disciples who inquired: "Why do the scribes say that Elias must come first?" He, answering, said to them: "Elias indeed shall come and restore all things." He then speaks of another Elias, who is clearly to be distinguished from the one that "shall come." "I say to you that Elias is already come, and they knew him not, but have done to him whatsoever they had a mind: so also the Son of Man shall suffer from them."[48] The Elias in regard to whom our Lord says that he "shall come" is the Thesbite; and the Elias in regard to whom He says that he "is already come" is John the Baptist, declared by the angel before his conception to be he that "shall convert many of the children of Israel to the Lord their God, and shall go before Him in the spirit and power of Elias."[49] Both Eliases mentioned by our Lord were His precursors. Elias the Thesbite is the herald of the second advent of Christ, the Baptist being the herald of the first.

In the Apocalypse there is a remarkable account of two "witnesses," or "prophets," who are to appear at the end of the world to be martyred, and after three days and a half to rise again and to ascend "up to heaven in a cloud."[50] That these two will be Henoch and Elias is the ancient and almost universal opinion of the fathers. So

[47] Mal. 4:6.
[48] Mt. 17:10, 12.
[49] Lk 1:16, 17.

204

Appendix

general has been the prevalence of this belief that Suarez unhesitatingly affirms it to be either of faith, or very proximate to faith.[51] He says that he can only discover three other persons who have ever been conjectured by any expositors as at all likely to correspond with the indication given in the Apocalypse, namely, Moses, Jeremias and St. John the Evangelist; and the probabilities against these are, to his mind, decisive upon the question.

The mission of Henoch and Elias will be to preach in sackcloth against Antichrist for "one thousand two hundred and sixty days"[52] The special office of Elias will be to convert all the Jews who will hear his word. This is what is meant by Malachi: "He shall turn the heart of the fathers to the children and the heart of the children to the fathers, lest I come and strike the earth with anathema."[53] This conversion was alluded to by our Lord when He said: "Elias shall indeed come and restore all things."[54] By "restoring all things" St. Chrysostom says that Christ means the return of the Jews from their unbelief just before His second advent,[55] lest all of them should perish. Elias will "turn the heart of the fathers to the children" when the descendants of their forefathers, the patriarchs, shall have in their souls the same faith which the patriarchs had possessed; for of Abraham it was declared by Jesus Christ Himself, "Abraham, your father, rejoiced that he might see My day: he saw it, and was glad."[56] Turning the "heart of the children to the

[50] Apoc. 11:3-12.
[51] Myst. Vit. Christi, lix, disp. iv, art. 6, sec. 2.
[52] Apoc. 11:3. 57
[53] Mal. iv. 6.
[54] Mt. 17:11.
[55] Hom. 57 al. 58 in Matt.

fathers" may be only another form of stating that the faith of those Jews who shall be converted at the end of the world shall be identical with that of the early Israelites, the faith of the children being conformable to that of the fathers. The same special object of the future coming of Elias is also manifestly indicated in the following allusion to him by name in the book of Ecclesiasticus: "Elias . . . who wast taken up in a whirlwind of fire in a chariot of fiery horses, who art registered in the judgments of times, to appease the wrath of the Lord, to reconcile the heart of the father to the son, and to restore the tribes of Jacob."[57] The reference to the tribes of Jacob reminds us of Elias on Mount Carmel, when he repaired the altar of the Lord and "took twelve stones, according to the number of the sons of Jacob."[58] Elias, by his ministry, will appease the wrath of the Lord because, if none were converted to faith and repentance, then God would be obliged, according to Malachi, to strike the earth, i.e., to destroy in His vengeance men who live on the earth, or, says St. Gregory, "those who mind earthly things." "Elias," says Tertullian, "is to come again, not from a state of departure from life, but of translation; nor is he to be restored to his body, for he has never yet been exempted from it; but he is to be given back to the world from which he was translated; not as if to return to the threshold of a life which he had left, but in fulfillment of prophecy (*non ex postliminio vitae, sed ex supplemento prophetiae*); he being the identical man himself, having the same name and personality (*idem et ipse, et sui nominis et sui hominis*)."[59]

[56] Jn. 8:56.
[57] Eccu. 48:10.
[58] 3Kngg 18:31.

Appendix

St. Augustine testifies strongly to the universal expectation of the Church in regard to Elias: "That in the last times before the judgment, the Jews, having had the Law expounded to them by this great and wonderful Elias, will become believers, is a truth most familiar to the hearts, and frequently spoken of in the discourses of the faithful (*celeberrimum est in sermonibus et cordibus fidelium*). Indeed, most worthily is it believed that Elias will come before the advent of the Savior and Judge; because worthily is it believed that he is now alive; since he was carried away in a fiery chariot from human things, as the Scripture bears witness."[60] As Suarez observes, the conversion of the Jews is to be the special work of Elias, and that of the Gentiles of Henoch; for which purpose these two prophets will be peculiarly adapted, Henoch, the "seventh from Adam," representing the uncircumcision, and Elias the circumcision. Henoch was translated that he may "give repentance to the nations,"[61] and Elias that he may restore the tribes of Israel.[62]

When Christ first came, says Suarez, into the world, His immediate purpose was to gather into His fold "the lost sheep of the house of Israel,"[63] and He had, therefore, only one forerunner, who was an Israelite, John the Baptist. But at His second advent He will send two, a Gentile and a Jew, because He will then come not to the Jews specially, but to His universal Church gathered out of both Jews and Gentiles. The period during which Henoch and Elias are to exercise their office is to be one thousand two hundred and sixty days; a space of time cor-

[59] De Anima, 35.
[60] De Civitate, lib. xx, c. 29.
[61] Ecclus. 44:16.
[62] Ecclus. 48:10.
[63] Mt. 15:24.

responding with the duration of Christ's public ministry, and also, as it will be remembered, with that of the judicial drought in the days of Achab, when Elias closed the heavens for "three years and six months."[64]

The garments in which the two prophets are to be clothed will be sackcloth, in order to show their austerity and poverty; also, says St. Thomas, to indicate that the Church in its old age will return to the day of its youth, when John the Baptist preached in a mantle of camel's hair. They are described, as "the two olive-trees," and the "two candlesticks that stand before the Lord." The former signifies their compassion, interior and exterior, and the latter, the light of their testimony by word and example — a light which they never fail to give forth, because, fearless of Antichrist, they "stand before the Lord," even if their bodies fall by death. So St. Thomas[65] with beautiful subtlety expounds the meaning of the above and other figurative allusions to Henoch and Elias. They will have immense supernatural powers, "if any man will hurt them, fire shall come out of their mouths and shall devour their enemies." They will also be able to "shut heaven," to turn water into blood, and to "strike the earth with all plagues as often as they will." They will probably, says Suarez, not always go together, but will travel separately through the world, consoling and teaching men by their writings as well as by speech. Some think that they will have disciples to assist them by a kind of apostolate. At length, Antichrist, "the beast that ascendeth out of the abyss," will be allowed by the will of God to "make war against them, overcome them and kill them." The place of their martyrdom will be Jerusalem, "the great city which is

[64] Lk. 4:25.
[65] Apoc. Ch 11

Appendix

called spiritually Sodom and Egypt, where their Lord also was crucified." For three days and a half their bodies "shall lie in the streets," to be gazed upon by all classes "of the tribes, and peoples, and tongues, and nations." They shall remain unburied, as St. Thomas observes, either from fear of Antichrist, or hatred of Henoch and Elias, or as a deterrent example to persons inclined to follow their teaching, or in order that, being seen dead by all eyes for three days and a half, their resurrection may thus be the more brilliant and convincing as a miraculous demonstration. Whilst their corpses lie exposed, "they that dwell upon the earth shall rejoice over them and make merry, and shall send gifts one to another, because these two prophets tormented them that dwelt upon the earth;" i.e., says St. Thomas, they "tormented" the worldly by predicting their future anguish and by resisting boldly their iniquity. When St. John, in the Apocalypse, describes their resurrection he suddenly changes the tense from the future to the present, as if his vision were too vivid to be otherwise narrated. "After three days and a half the spirit of life from God entered into them and they stood upon their feet, and great fear fell upon them that saw them; and they heard a great voice from heaven saying to them, 'Come up hither:' and they went up in a cloud, and their enemies saw them; and at that hour there was made a great earthquake, and the tenth part of the city fell; and there were slain in the earthquake names of men seven thousand; and the rest were cast into a fear, and gave glory to the God of heaven."[66]

To the question as to whether their risen bodies were glorified so that they could never again die, or were only

---

[66] Apoc. xi, 11-13.

temporarily quickened like the body of Lazarus, the answer is that they were glorified like the body of Christ. The soul that entered them was a soul vivified by the divine virtue, not by its own nature.[67] If it be argued, says the Angelic Doctor, that this would be contrary to St. Paul, who, speaking of the patriarchs,[68] declares that they could not receive "the promise" (i.e., of a "better resurrection") "without us," namely until the general resurrection, he replies that a glorious resurrection was given to them beforehand, as a special privilege, and moreover, that in point of time the anticipation would be very brief. Though their bodies were glorified, "their enemies saw them" without the aid of a miracle, because it is a property of such bodies that they can, at will, be visible or invisible. "It was just that they who had imitated Christ in preaching and tribulation should be conformed to Him in His ascension; and because by first humbling themselves in sackcloth and by being slain, they descended; therefore, worthily are they said to ascend."[69] The animal body is identical with the spiritual, observes St. Epiphanius, alluding to the risen body of Christ, but with this distinction, that the spirit changes that very body into its own tenuity and subtleness, and so blends it with itself as to make it altogether spiritual.[70]

The death, resurrection and ascension of Henoch and Elias will be speedily followed by the ruin of Antichrist, "whom the Lord Jesus will kill with the spirit of His mouth, and shall destroy with the brightness of His coming."[71] So close will be the destruction of Antichrist upon

[71] St. Thom. in loc. cit.
[72] Heb. 11:5-10, 35.
[73] St. Thom. loc. cit.
[74] Adv. Haer. lib. ii, xliv, al. lxiv, s. 64.

Appendix

the martyrdoms of Henoch and Elias, that in the words of
Tertullian, "they are reserved in order that they may
extinguish him by their blood."[72] According to St. Thomas,
the death of Antichrist will precede their resurrection.
"*Verum est quod surrexerunt quarta die post interfectionem suam
mortuo prius Antichristo*"; but according to the more general
calculation, Antichrist will survive for thirty days afterwards. He is to reign "a time, times and half a time."[73] If a
time means a year, the period will be equivalent to the
"thousand and ninety days" mentioned by Daniel as the
duration of the "abomination unto desolation,"[74] and the
witnesses will prophesy for "a thousand two hundred and
sixty days."

4. *The meaning of (a) Luke, 1:17; (b) John, 1:21, 25; (c)
Luke, 9 :7, 8, 54-56; (d) Matthew, 27 :47-49.*

(a) Luke 1:17. "He shall convert many of the children of
Israel to the Lord their God, and he shall go before Him in
the spirit and power of Elias, that he may turn the hearts
of the fathers unto the children."

These words were spoken by the angel Gabriel to
Zachary when prophetically announcing to him the birth
of John the Baptist: "Thy wife Elizabeth shall bear thee a
son, and thou shalt call his name John."[75] There are various interpretations of the expressions "spirit and power."
By some commentators "spirit" is considered to mean the
Holy Ghost: "he shall be filled with the Holy Ghost even
from his mother's womb:"[76] and "power" is held to signify

[71] 2Thes. 2:8.
[72] De Anima, 50.
[73] Dan. 7:5.
[74] xii, 11, Cornel, a Lapide, in Apoc. xi, 3, and Dan. in loc.; also
Suarez Myst. v Christi, q. lix, disp. Iv, s. 2 d.
[75] Lk. 1:13.

211

The Prophet of Carmel

his office and ministry. Toletus adopts the opinion of St. Gregory,[77] according to which "spirit" is equivalent to office. He observes that "in spirit and power" means with spirit and power; just as it is declared that Christ will come in a cloud with great power and majesty.[78] John shall therefore go before Christ with the spirit and power of Elias. The word "spirit" is often used for the gift and office of the Holy Ghost; thus we read of the "spirit" of prophecy, knowledge, evangelizing; and St. Paul speaks of his apostleship as his "spirit." Hence John is described as having the spirit of the Thesbite, because like him he was to be a precursor of Christ, though in respect to a different advent. By "power," Toletus does not believe that there is any allusion to miraculous signs. John, he remarks with St. Chrysostom, did no miracle, probably lest the people, who believed in him without miracles, might have mistaken him for the Messias. The "power of Elias," with which John was invested, refers to his zeal, his holy vehemence, the effectiveness of his preaching, the sanctity of his life and the bold freedom with which he fulfilled his ministry.

Alluding to the words "he will go before Him," Tertullian explains that John will not go with the soul and body of Elias, for these are the essences (*substantiae*) of each individual man; but "spirit and power" will be conferred upon him extrinsically, by the favor of God, since they can be transferred to another.[79]

The likeness of spirit and power between John and the Thesbite does not consist in certain analogous circum-

[76] Lk. 1:17. 81 Hom. vii, in Evang.
[77] Hom. vii, in Evang.
[78] Lk. 21:27.
[79] De Anima, 35.

stances of their career, as, for instance, that both of them rebuked kings, wore austere garments, were zealous for the law, lived much in solitude and were persecuted. Resemblances like these are true, but the Baptist, according to that interpretation, would be compared with the past Elias of the days of Achab, rather than with the Elias who is to come again as the precursor of Christ. Yet the language of the angel to Zachary clearly points to an identity of office and ministry between the two, which is not evident unless the allusion is to the return of the Thesbite at the end of the world, when he will prepare men, and the Jews more especially, for the coming of Christ.[80] Our Lord distinguishes between the precursor who had already come and the precursor who "shall come," and at the same time declares their similarity by calling them both by the mutual name of Elias.[81] "Christ called John "Elias" not because he was Elias in person, but because he fulfilled the same ministry."[82] It is worthy of observation, that the angel in declaring that John would convert many of the children to the Lord their God, and that he would go before Him in the spirit and power of Elias, proclaims the divinity of Jesus Christ.

(b) John 1:21. "They asked him, 'What then? Art thou Elias?' and he said, "I am not.'"

How can this reply of the Baptist to the Pharisees, in which he denies that he is Elias, be reconciled with the declaration of Christ affirming that he was Elias? "All the prophets and the Law prophesied until John, and if you will receive it, he is Elias that is to come,"[83] referring to Malachi 4:5, "Behold, I send My angel, and he shall pre-

---

[80] Compare St. Luke I, 17, with Mal. 4:6.

[81] St. Matt. xvii, 11.

[82] St. Chrysos. Hom. lvii, al. lviii, in Matt.

pare the way before My face." (Malachi iii:1) And again: "Elias is already come, and they knew him not, but have done unto him whatsoever they had a mind,"[84] in allusion to John's decapitation by Herod. The explanation of this apparent contradiction between the Baptist and our Lord is that John addressed himself to the minds of the Pharisees, who thought that he might be Elias the Thesbite in person, an impression which his austere garment of camel's hair would favor. He, therefore, answered truly that he was not Elias, in their sense of the name. He did not tell them that he might be justly called Elias, the precursor of Christ, because, out of humility, he abstained from using any laudatory epithet in regard to himself; and because the object of the Pharisees was not to know the truth, but to catch him in his words. When Christ explained how John was Elias, He was satisfying the legitimate curiosity of His disciples, Peter, James and John, who had just beheld Elias the Thesbite on the Mount of Transfiguration, a wonderful fact which no doubt suggested to them the question: "Why do the Scribes and Pharisees say that Elias must come first?"[85]

(b) John 1:25. "They (the Pharisees) asked him (John the Baptist), and said to him, Why, then, dost thou baptize, if thou be not Christ, nor Elias, nor the prophet?"

The Jews, especially those of them who were learned like the Pharisees, connected the idea of baptism with the coming of the Messias. They were familiar with the prophecy of Ezekiel: "I will pour upon you clean water, and you shall be cleansed from all your sins."[86] And they also knew that there was no ceremonial law equivalent to

[87] Mt. 11:10-14.
[88] Mt. 17:12.
[89] Mk. 9: 9, 10.

214

Appendix

the baptism of repentance which they saw John administering, and that to no prophet had this office ever been assigned before. When, therefore, they found that John denied being either the Christ, or Elias, or the prophet, they imagined that they had convicted him of doing a religious act which was utterly unlawful, except at the time of the coming of Christ, which event they did not believe had arrived. Elias is mentioned because they connected him with the advent of Christ, and probably thought that he or the prophet[87] would baptize as the ministers of the Messias, either immediately preceding or accompanying him. As the Pharisees had no distinct idea of two advents of Christ, so they had no idea of two kinds of baptism, that of John "in water" only, and that of Christ "in the Holy Ghost."[88]

(c) Luke 9:7, 8. "It was said by some that John was risen from the dead: but by others that Elias had appeared, and by others that one of the old prophets was risen again."

These words are the answer made to Herod when he was wondering who Christ could be. Elias is said to have "appeared," whilst the others are spoken of as having risen from the dead. It has been well observed that the expression "appear" shows the universal belief of the Jews that Elias was still alive and expected to return.

(c) Luke 9:54-6. 'Lord, wilt Thou that we command fire to come down from heaven and consume them?' And turning, He rebuked them, saying: 'Ye know not of what spirit you are. The Son of Man came not to destroy, but to save.'

James and John, who had been called the "sons of thunder"[89] by our Lord Himself, wished, in imitation of Elias,[90]

[86] Ez. 36:25.
[87] In allusion perhaps to Deut. 18:15.
[88] Mt. 3:11.

215

to destroy by fire those Samaritans who refused to receive Christ into their city. It is rather a singular coincidence that the soldiers whom Elias consumed were "messengers of the king of Samaria."[91]

Our Lord, in reproving those disciples for their mistaken mode of showing zeal for His honor, intended not so much to blame as to instruct them, still less did He intend to imply that Elias had been at fault. "Let no one imagine," says St. Chrysostom, "that we blame Elias as being imperfect. We affirm nothing of the kind, for he was an exceedingly perfect man; but this was in his own times, when the intelligence of men was more puerile and required this kind of schooling."[92]

"Ye know not of what spirit you are," i.e., you do not perceive that you are influenced by impatience and vindictiveness on account of yourselves as well as Me. You do not understand that the kingdom of the Spirit is gentleness compared to the spirit of the Old Law, when it was "eye for eye and tooth for tooth."[93] Christ wished also to explain to them that His special object at His first coming was not to slay those who would not receive Him, but if possible to win them by love. "Those Samaritans," observes Bede, "who were saved in this place from the fiery destruction believed the more quickly."[94]

Christ did not intend to condemn, as a principle of the Gospel, every act of external punishment without exception. St. Peter struck Ananias and Sapphira dead,[95] and St. Paul delivered a Corinthian to "Satan for the destruction of the

[89] Mk. 3:17.
[90] 4Kng. 1:10-12.
[91] 4Kng. 5:3.
[92] Hom. in Matt. lvii, al. lviii.
[93] Ex. 21:24.
[94] St. Thom. "Catena Aurea," in Luke 9

flesh,"[96] and smote Elymas with blindness.[97] As there was sometimes severity under the New Dispensation, so there was sometimes clemency under the Old. Eliseus, instead of allowing the Syrians who had come in great force to take him captive, set a "great provision of meats before them," and sent them back unharmed to their master.[98] The distinction therefore between the severity of the Law and the kindness of the Gospel was not so perpetual as to admit of no exception.[99]

To the charge sometimes made against Elias that he was culpable for consuming men by fire, Theodoret thus replies: "They who accuse the prophet speak against God, for He it was who sent down the fire. It is, indeed, an act of excessive audacity to be angry at the administration of God; for men ought to know that the equity of His divine providence consists in punishing sinners, and in rewarding with kindness those who worship him."[100]

(d)Matt. 27:47-49. "This man calleth Elias. And immediately one of them running took a sponge, and filled it with vinegar; and put it on a reed, and gave Him to drink. And the others said, Let be; let us see whether Elias will come to deliver him."

These words were spoken after our dying Lord had "cried with a loud voice, saying: Eli, Eli, lamma sabacthani? that is, My God, My God, why hast Thou forsaken me?" Whether the speakers were Roman soldiers[101] who, from long residence in Jerusalem, had learned the Jewish tradition about Elias, but, being ignorant of Hebrew, mis-

[95] Acts 5:1-10.
[96] 1Cor. 5:5.
[97] Acts 13:11.
[98] 4Kng. 6:23.
[99] Beda ap. Maldonatus.
[100] Inter. xv, in 4Kng.
[101] Lk. 23:36; Jn. 19:29.

The Prophet of Carmel

took our Lord's words, or whether they were Jews, it is not easy to determine.

On the hypothesis that they were Jews, were they some of the unlettered rabble who stood near the cross, or were they erudite scribes and Pharisees? The most probable opinion seems to be that they were men who knew perfectly well what our Lord was exclaiming, and in mocking derision pretended that Christ, in the desperation of His agony, was invoking Elias. Perhaps, as there were several who uttered the words, one catching them up from another, the speakers would attach to them various meanings according to their state of knowledge and disposition of heart.

There is something appalling in the circumstance that the Jews, by alluding to Elias, were confessing their faith in the Messias, whilst they were actually putting Him to death. Many centuries have passed since then, yet, as it has been well observed, the Jews are to this day under the same delusion, and, with the knowledge of Calvary before them, are ever vainly saying: "Let be; let us see whether Elias will come."

Laus Deo Virginique Matri!